Life Without . . . My Father

by

The son I became

The following story is based closely on true events.

Names and places have been changed throughout to preserve the anonymity of the people involved. We have each dealt with these events in our own way and wish to continue to do so.

In dedication to my only love
Maggie

I did it for friends, for family
I did it for Queen, for country
And by the grace of God
I did it for Saint George

And for you
Clare

It's said that time heals all wounds, but I disagree. Over time, the mind and body will try to cover its' wounds to protect itself. The pain may lessen, but the memories are always there.

Dave Baily

Chapter 1
Life Without . . . Mum

I was born in Bedfordshire towards the end of 1970, and from what I've been told I was taken to Yorkshire soon after. The family returned to Bedfordshire two years later, for the birth of my sister, Sarah. Also with us were my two older stepbrothers, Russell, eight, and Adrian, six, both from Mum's previous marriage.

Most of my early childhood memories are vague, but not this one: during the summer of '76, the hottest summer on record at the time, I was in the paddling pool that Dad got for us to cool off in; I must have fallen asleep there without anyone noticing and got sunburnt.

That day the sun had been so intense I ended up with a second-degree burn on my back. I remember the pain from the dry skin, but I think more of the cooling lotion Mum gently rubbed over my back, and Dad running about unable to get enough ice cream for me. That is a fond memory of childhood, but fond memories are few and far apart. The following year, Mum and Dad started to have problems.

I don't remember many arguments between them, but the day Dad walked out with his bags I cried for him to come back. Then, as I watched Mum throw away anything he'd left behind, I blamed myself for their problems – as a young boy pushing seven this was the natural thing to do, I suppose.

Dad came back every few days over the coming weeks to talk with Mum, and before he left each night he'd always say that things would get better soon. It didn't stop me feeling unloved after he'd gone, and I would cry myself to sleep.

Then one day, as Dad was walking up the path, Mum started shouting about how she hated him coming to the house anymore. She opened the door and told him that he wasn't coming in. A barrage of insults was thrown both ways as he asked to see us kids until she slammed the door in his face.

I was allowed to cry my goodbyes' through the letterbox before Dad told me to stand back. He punched out one of the glass panels in the front door and went for the latch. As he was fumbling with the doorknob, Adrian came out of nowhere and grabbed his arm, putting all his weight on Dad's wrist; Russell, then Mum, soon joined him.

With all three of them hanging from his arm, Dad didn't stand a chance. They pulled it down onto the jagged glass still sticking up from the frame, and dragged it from side to side, leaving a really bad gash across his wrist. I tried as hard as I could to get them off Dad but they were too strong.

With blood everywhere, Dad's hand became slippery, so they eventually lost grip, and as everyone else fell backwards, I found myself still standing. Seconds later, I opened the door and chased after Dad, begging to go with him, but as I was running down the path, Adrian pushed me onto the grass.

I stumbled, but looked up in time to see the cricket bat Adrian was wielding come down on Dad's head. One step later, I regained my balance and dived for Dad's falling body, grabbing onto his back in the hope of protecting him in some way. Then Mum came screaming something as she grabbed Adrian and dragged him back into the house.

Dad started to get to his feet with a little help and encouragement from me, but on his way to the car he fell again. He was bleeding badly and barely conscious now; I even started to think he might be dying. I was screaming as loud as I could for someone to help, and the strong hand of a neighbour answered my cry.

After making sure I was okay, our neighbour put a makeshift tourniquet above the cut. Though Dad didn't really have his senses about him, but he allowed himself to be led away to hospital anyway.

I wanted to go with them, but Mum insisted they wouldn't be there long. Then a few hours later our neighbour came back to say Dad had been stitched up and was fine, but he wouldn't come back to the house any time soon.

Dad did come back a few times over the next week or two, but he was afraid of coming to the door. Instead, he would park in front of the house and wait for Sarah and me to go to the car instead.

We never went anywhere, just sat there for an hour or so talking, until Mum came out to get us. She would then have a few minutes with Dad before he left again.

About a month after Dad's hospital visit, I was lying in bed when I heard him calling my name. I jumped out of bed and looked out of the window for him. I was still a little sleepy so, I couldn't work out why he wasn't on the garden path. Then he called again and I realised he was in the room next to mine.

I ran into my parents' bedroom and jumped on the bed, landing on top of Dad, there next to Mum. Sarah joined us a few minutes later and we couldn't stop saying how happy we were that Mum and Dad had worked things out and we were going to be a family again.

The week that followed Dad picked me up from

school every day. Back at home he would let me choose what I wanted for dinner before I woke Mum ready for her night shift. Then the evenings were filled with talk of trips to see friends and relatives, or play-fighting with my older brothers.

Dad had promised to take us to see an old friend of his that weekend. He had a lovely family, and their children all a similar ages to us. Sometimes we would all go out collecting berries for his wife to make into jam; then, with bread made fresh that day, our first taste would empty the jar, leaving nothing to take home. These visits had once been a regular thing, but with everything going on it had been months since our last trip.

Excited about the visit when I woke that Saturday, I ran around the house getting things ready. Then at around nine o'clock I went to wake Dad, but he wasn't there. Mum stirred, so I asked her where he was. Sleepily, she told me that he had gone to get his things to move back in properly. I was even more excited now that Dad was really coming back, and woke Sarah to give her the good news.

Dad must have got the shock of his life when he came back later that afternoon, with two kids running to hug his legs. He picked us up, one in each arm, kissing us all the while. Then Mum walked past with her bags and got into a waiting taxi without saying a word to anyone.

As the taxi pulled away, it dawned on me in the cold light of day, that it was Mum who wasn't coming back this time. Dad tried to explain that there was no more love between him and Mum, and it didn't matter how much I asked, they would never share the same house again.

After my tears quietened down he went on to tell me, that she would be staying locally with a friend of hers, and though I couldn't go there to visit, she would still take me and Sarah out at weekends until she found her own place.

Visits from Mum were rare from the start, but she phoned often to talk to each of us in turn. Then a few weeks went past without us hearing anything from her, so I asked Dad what was going on.

"Oh, she's got some fancy-man with her now and doesn't want you lot getting in the way of her love life," Dad told me.

I was devastated, and phoned Mum to see if it was true. She admitted she did have a new boyfriend, but had never said that she didn't want to see Sarah or me, blaming everything on Dad for not wanting to take us to her. I didn't know whom to believe but, I suppose I sided more with Dad because of the lack of visits we had had since Mum left. I rarely saw her after that.

Adrian was about eleven by then, and probably took the news about Mum's boyfriend worse than the rest of us. He really didn't want to stay with his stepfather, Dad, and began to be very difficult. He would start fights, and bunked off school so much that they expelled him in the end.

Dad went into a rage like I had never seen before and shouted for Adrian to get to his room. They were yelling at each other at the top of their voices, and then I heard Adrian scream in pain. Dad had pulled him over his knee by the hair, then taking his slipper off, started to smack him with it.

The smacks came so quick it was impossible to keep count. Everything quietened down soon after, and Dad went back downstairs. Seconds later, Adrian ran down the stairs and out of the front door. The police brought him back two days later, after finding him trying to jump on a train to London.

Out of school, Adrian also fell in with the wrong crowd and would get brought home by the police night after night for fighting or having been found drunk somewhere. Dad did try to get some control over him with the slipper, but Adrian would just laugh. Then one day Dad tried using a four-by-two-inch plank. Adrian got it off him somehow and then chased him down the road with it.

After that, Dad sent him to Mum for her to sort out. She did no better, and nor did his real father when he tried. Eventually, getting caught for some minor crime, Adrian ended up in Borstal before his thirteenth birthday.

Once Adrian had left the family home, Dad got a job as a taxi driver working late evenings and nights, leaving Russell to look after Sarah and me. He would have been about thirteen then, and talked about joining the Army as soon as he was old enough. He wanted to train to be a chef, and was generally a good kid doing well at school; but every now and again he would do something wrong, as kids do, and get a few smacks from the slipper.

After a few weeks of babysitting Sarah and me, Russell started to bring his girlfriend round to keep him company. Then one evening, Dad came home early, and went ballistic, finding the two of them sitting together watching TV. The screaming match between them went on for hours after Russell's girlfriend left. All I remember of it is Dad shouting that if she ever came back Russell was going to get the beating of his life.

After that, Russell would sometimes pop to his girlfriend's house, leaving me to look after Sarah for an hour or so. Then one day a police officer knocked on the door while he was out. When the officer asked where Dad was, I gave him the taxi firm's number, and then he asked who was sitting for us.

I told him Russell had just gone to the shops, and volunteered to go and hurry him up. The officer let me run off, and not long later I came back with Russell in tow. I went out to play then, leaving them alone to talk.

In the early hours of that night I was woken by an almighty crash, followed by shouting and another crash, as Russell was thrown across the living room again. It seemed to go on for an eternity; then I heard Sarah screaming, so I went to find her.

She was hiding in her bedroom, and we huddled down in the corner together, staying there until a couple of doors were slammed shut and everything went quiet. Then I heard footsteps on the stairs, and I became terrified as the bedroom door opened.

"Dave, you in here?" It was Russell. I stood up from behind the bed so we could see each other.

He looked in a right state as blood flowed down his shirt from his broken nose, and his eyes were so swollen I would be surprised if he could see me at all. He also had a missing tooth and two broken ribs, as I later found out.

"He's kicked me out," Russell mumbled, struggling through his fat lips. "It's up to you now, look after Sarah."

"What?" I asked, turning to Sarah, who was still curled up crying on the floor.

"I'm leaving. Everything is yours now, okay?" he said, turning towards the door, "I'll still be keeping an eye on you both, but…,"

Russell closed the door behind him, never finishing the sentence. I stayed with Sarah for a few minutes, before I went to find him, but I was too late: Russell had left taking almost nothing with him.

The following morning the same police officer called so I woke Dad and they had a chat about Adrian. He had run off from Borstal and had been seen in the area, and they had thought he might be staying at our house, but he never did.

Without Russell to babysit us, it soon became clear that

Dad had lost his job. He'd crashed one of the taxis going the wrong way down a one-way street. Instead of working, he had been going out with friends and had met someone, and one night soon after, we met his new girlfriend.

Kelly was a few years younger than Dad and seemed nice enough. She had three kids of her own that we would see often now. Dean was a few months younger than me, Suzanne was about Sarah's age, and she also had a new-born, Sally. They lived just around the corner, and as Kelly was splitting from her husband who still lived there, she would stay with us almost every night now, bringing the baby.

Their romance soon blossomed and the day Kelly's divorce papers came through, Dad proposed and she accepted. I remember the wedding was held on a Thursday, because I had to go to school and didn't go to the ceremony, but Russell picked me up after school to get ready for the reception.

The party went well, with lots of fun and games for everyone; then Russell took Sarah and me home. On the way, he said he would be looking after us for a few days so Dad and Kelly could enjoy their honeymoon. They came back late in the night on Saturday.

The following morning, Dad shouted that he wanted a cup of tea made for him. Russell had already left by then, but I had been up for hours, so I called back saying it was on its way and put the kettle on. As I gathered the tea things together, I could see there wasn't going to be enough milk, so I called up again to say I was off to the shops.

The shops weren't that far and I ran all the way, as fast as a boy just turned seven could. So, with re-boiling the kettle, I think it took me about twenty minutes to be stood outside Dad's bedroom, with two piping hot drinks.

After kicking the door open gently, I was about to say

something to the happy newlyweds when something hard hit me on the back of the head. The shock of the impact sent me stumbling forwards, spilling the scalding drinks down the front of my trousers.

I didn't know what hurt more, my legs or my head, when Dad's belt buckle hit me again, this time on the back of the neck and, I fell to the floor.

"What took you so fucking long?" he shouted.

"There was no milk!" I called back, rolling over and putting my hand over my face in case he swung again. Dad shouted something at me so loud I couldn't understand him. Then I rolled back over, intending to get up, but Kelly came from around the bed.

"What's that shit doing on my floor?" she screamed, and put her foot on the back of my head, pushing my face into the carpet. "Lick it up, you dirty little fucker!"

Then she forced my face into the floor so hard that I could barely breathe. When she finally let me up, she grabbed the neck of my T-shirt and threw me out of the room.

Dad had never hit me before and I didn't want him to again, so, when he and Kelly got up a short time later, I knew I would have to be on my very best behaviour. I was shouted at a lot for the rest of the day, but my only real punishment was to make all the drinks for them.

Later that evening, while I was sharing a bath with Sarah, Dad came upstairs and saw me holding a flannel over my face. I said it was part of a game I was playing with Sarah, but it was obvious to him that I had been crying. He knelt down next to the bath, and after wiping away a tear, he said, "Well, that's what you get for telling us to fuck off and make our own tea."

"I didn't say that, honest Dad. I would never say a swear word to anyone, and I like making the tea for you," I pleaded.

"Then why is your step mum telling me you swore this morning son?" Dad asked.

"I didn't Dad, I said that I'm off for some milk, I'll be about ten, to the shops. Don't you remember, Dad, we needed some more milk?" I sobbed, praying he would believe me.

He admitted he had heard me call something, but couldn't make out what it was. Then he wanted to know exactly what I had said, and as near as I could remember I recalled it word for word for him.

Dad thought for a few moments in silence, before telling me to get out the bath. The room was tiny so, after drying my feet, I wrapped the towel around myself and headed for my bedroom to dry off.

"The thing is Dave," Dad said as I left the room. I stopped at my bedroom door and turned towards him before he continued. "Kelly went to check that you were okay and says there was plenty of milk, but you had already run off. And I'll tell you this for nothing, what she tells me you said and what you say don't sound anything alike. Now, she's got no reason to lie about you, so tell me why I shouldn't tan your hide right now?"

"I'm not saying she's lying, just she didn't hear me properly Dad. Please believe me," I begged, and started to cry.

Dad nodded, then closed the bathroom door. Seconds later Sarah's screams filled the house as she had her hair washed. They never lasted long, and after a few minutes of playtime to calm her back down she came to my room, followed by Dad.

"Right Dave, I know you're not telling me the whole truth. The only reason I'm not smacking your arse now is because I have to sort her out." Dad gestured towards Sarah, who was still dripping wet. "But let this be a warning to you: and if I ever hear you swear I'll clout you so hard you'll still feel it next week. Got it!"

I nodded to show I'd understood.

"Now, say goodnight to your sister, and I don't want

to hear from you again tonight," he said, nudging Sarah a little closer to me.

I didn't want to be in any more trouble than I was already in, so, after hugging Sarah goodnight, I climbed into bed and cried myself to sleep. I did my best to help out after school in the days that followed, and soon all seemed to be forgiven.

Chapter 2

Dean and Suzanne had been staying with their dad before the wedding, but now, as a married woman again, Kelly wanted all of her family under the same roof. Shouting matches across the garden between Kelly and her ex-husband soon became a daily occurrence as a custody battle started. Kelly won sole custody in the end, with her ex moving back to Ireland to get away from her, so Dean and Suzanne joined us in the house.

As the others moved in Kelly decided that she didn't want any kids messing about in the living room when we had visitors, so, the dining room became the den for us. Sally's cot and Suzanne were moved into Sarah's large bedroom, with our parents in the master bedroom. This left Dean and me to share the smallest room in the house. We had a built-in cupboard to share as a wardrobe, but after bunk beds were moved in, there wasn't much room for anything else.

I had got on okay with Dean so far, so when he asked to have the bottom bunk I didn't argue. As we settled in together over the coming weeks I noticed Dean would turn his mattress over every couple of days. I didn't really think too much of it until I climbed out of bed one morning.

There wasn't enough room for the ladder to the top bunk, so I used Dean's bunk as a step. I put my foot on his mattress, and it was soaked. I jumped down and pulled the bed covers off him, and seeing him there, on a soaking wet sheet, told me why he turned his mattress so often.

Dad was already up, so I went and told him what had happened; he started shouting at Dean, waking Kelly up. As she came into the room, Dean started crying, saying I had got up in the night and peed on him.

Kelly went off on one at me, calling me a "lying,

dirty, little shit" amongst other things, and that must be the case because her boy hadn't wet the bed since he was two or something. Then Dad gave me a clout round the ear for telling tales, and said I would have to sleep on the bottom bunk until I had learned my lesson.

I flipped the mattress, but Dean had soaked it right through so the underside was just as bad as the top; I opted to sleep on the floor instead that night. A couple of nights later, Kelly caught me bedding down under the bed and made me get into the bottom bunk. She then checked on me every hour or so until she went to bed herself. By then though the mattress had had time to dry, well almost, so I used plenty of blankets to sleep on top of as well as under, and it wasn't too bad really.

A few nights later, I woke up with a drip hitting my face: Dean had done it again. It was the middle of the night this time so I dragged him off the top bunk and started to shout at him, waking Dad and Kelly, who were soon splitting us up.

Dean tried saying that he had wet the bed because he was scared of waking me up if he'd gone to the toilet. He spent the rest of that night on the sofa in the den. The following morning he had to take his mattress into the front garden to hose it down.

Dean's bed-wetting carried on, along with his trips to the front garden with his mattress. It soon became such a regular thing that the neighbours started to ask questions. Then Kelly would shout at me for not waking him up, knowing Dean had a weak bladder.

Then Dean came up with an idea that if he had an incentive he would be able to wake himself up during the night if he needed. So he told his mum that if she paid him twenty pence he wouldn't wet the bed.

I couldn't believe it when she agreed. I had never been given pocket money, and now he was going to get some for not being disgusting. That night, he asked me to wake him every hour; but I declined, even when he offered me half his earnings.

Dean managed to keep his bed dry that night, getting his reward of a shiny new coin in the morning, and carried on with the scheme for a few months. He didn't succeed every night, but his trips to the garden with mattress in tow became less frequent. It went on until Kelly brought him a plastic mattress and refused to pay him anymore.

Dean didn't like that, not least because waking up in a puddle of pee is a lot different to sleeping on a damp mattress. It didn't stop him wetting the bed though.

Money had been tight since Dad lost his job as a taxi driver, so when we needed clothes he and Kelly would go scrounging from their few friends. Anything they couldn't get from them would come from charity shops.

After these trips, Dad and Kelly would come back with a few black bags and dump the contents on the den floor for us to choose. The girls were about the same size and they got on well so, they tended to share everything, but I hadn't got on with Dean since he moved in.

I was a similar build to him, so when the clothes arrived we argued over everything. This would end up bringing Kelly into the room, and Dean would then get first choice. I was normally left with nothing that fitted, let alone in good condition.

At school, the poor state of my clothes made me a target for the bullies, and the situation wasn't made any better by Dean's arrival at the same school. He made sure that anyone that hadn't already guessed that my clothes were hand-me-downs knew where they'd come from, as well as spreading other rumours about me.

Most of the bullying at that time was just name-calling, with the occasional minor scuffle – nothing serious, more pushing each other around than fighting. I did try to fight back if things got too physical, but, bullies being bullies, I was nearly always outnumbered and I would come out worse off, with another rip or two added to my already tattered clothes.

One person who always stood up for me though was Andy Frost. He lived about a mile or so from my house and passed on his way to school; and so, safety being in numbers, I stayed close to him most of the time. Even after school, I would normally walk to his house and stay for an hour before going home.

Andy asked a few times why I would never invite him into my place. I never told him, but the truth was because I wasn't allowed to have friends round the house. And even if I were, there would be nothing to do anyway. My bedroom smelt like a public toilet, and in the den Dean ruled, or he would tell his Mum that I had said something to get me into trouble.

A few weeks into the spring term at school, I was hanging about with Andy during lunch break as normal, when almost every kid on the playground ran to the fence. At first I couldn't see why, but then Andy pointed out a camera crew filming some dogs. I don't remember what the story was about, but that night it was on the news.

I was chuffed to see myself on the television, walking across the middle of the playground, but when I got home that night Dad was waiting in the kitchen.

"So what you been up to today then son?" Dad asked, and I went through my day. "So you didn't see the cameras then, 'eh?" he asked when I'd finished, tilting his head.

"Yeah, I saw them," I said, "but they was outside the school and there was too many people to see what they was filming."

"Not too many to stop you showing your arse off though!" He lowered his tone and I could feel the anger in his voice.

"I didn't! Who told you that?" I already knew the

answer.

"Dean saw you!" he told me, as I expected. "Well, if you can show your arse to the whole world, you can get it out again now! Bend over!"

I didn't take my trousers down at first so had to be told again. This time, Dad shouted so loud in my ear that I went deaf for a minute or so. Then he held me by the back of the neck so I was bent over at ninety degrees, my trousers and underwear around my ankles, and he smacked me six or seven times. I lost count, because I was so close to the larder; every time he hit my bum my head hit the door. He followed that with a week's grounding.

The smacks hurt for a little while and I had a headache for a few hours, but seeing Dean walking about all evening with a smirk on his face made me feel worse. I knew if I said anything I would be called a liar, so I kept my mouth shut and stayed out of everyone's way, not leaving my room for the rest of the night.

The next day at school I told Andy what had happened. He offered to have a word with Dean, but I asked him not to. He found him alone at some point later and took him to one side anyway. Andy told me he only gave him a warning not to tell lies about me, but Dean insisted that he had been hit when he got home.

When I got in that evening, Kelly called me into the living room. She slapped me round the face and started screaming something, but because of the ringing in my ear I didn't catch too much of it. Then she added a week onto my grounding and gave me a list of chores.

They were nothing unusual – do the washing up, clean the bathroom, toilet, stuff like that – but I could never do them well enough to pass Kelly's constant inspections, so everything had to be done time and time again. Often she would keep me working until well into the early hours before I was finally allowed to sleep. When I told Andy the trouble he'd caused, he said he felt guilty, and offered to do some of my chores. I settled for him not trying to help me out again.

Dean was forever trying to get me into trouble after that. The most common thing he would do was tell his mum that he'd heard me swearing. She would tell Dad, who would call me to the living room to explain myself.

The more I pleaded my innocence, the louder Dad would shout until I was ordered to "Get here!" Then over his knees I got smacked until I said I was sorry, and was sent back to my chores or off to my room to think about what I'd done.

Another of Dean's favourite things to do was to leave a mess in the den before he went to school. Once he made it so bad I was half an hour late arriving. The headmaster wanted to see me when I did eventually arrive, and I was told off for being late, then he said that he would be writing a letter to Dad about it.

I'd been told to collect the letter from his secretary before I went home that afternoon. And after panicking all day, she told me that the head had been called away on business and hadn't mentioned anything about a letter. So that evening, I opened the back door, thinking I'd got away with it, and walked straight onto Dad's fist as he punched me in the face.

"Think you can be late for school and then mess up my fucking kitchen, do you!" he shouted, and punched me in the chest, sending me to the floor gasping for air. Leaving me in agony, he turned and walked out the room.

It was a minute or two before I got back on my feet and started looking for the mess. There was a bit of washing up on the side from Dad and Kelly's lunch, but that would be my first chore of the evening. The only other thing out of place was the blood oozing from my nose onto the floor.

I started to clean up the blood, but as fast as I cleaned

more dripped on the floor. So I put some tissue up my nose, and got on and cleaned up. Leaving the few dishes on the draining board, I spent the next hour in the bathroom until my nose had stopped bleeding.

I had a sharp pain in my chest and struggled to breathe for the rest of the night. But that didn't get me out of doing the washing up after everyone else had eaten, so with a shout from Kelly I was back in the kitchen after dinner.

Washing the dishes wasn't really that bad as long as I kept my elbows tucked into my chest, but I couldn't lift my arms above my shoulders without a lot of pain, so I carried the plates to where they were to be stored a few at a time. When all the dishes were finally stacked, I tried to get the first one into the high cupboard, but the pain from my chest was so intense I dropped it.

"You alright, son?" Dad asked, coming into the kitchen behind me.

"Sorry Dad, I couldn't help it," I replied. I think he could tell how scared I was because his look changed instantly.

"Look, get this shit cleared up and don't break any more plates, right? Once you're done, get out of here and I'll make sure she leaves you alone for a day or two, okay?" He said, then made a drink for himself, before going back to the living room.

I struggled along, putting the rest of the dishes away. Once Dad had left the room, I climbed on the side to make things easier for myself. Then broken rib or not, as soon as I was done, I was out of the house.

I went to Andy's that night but I didn't want to hang around his street, so we opted for going to the park instead. At least there I could keep my black eyes away from most people until I could think of a story for how I might have got them.

Andy never actually asked what happened, but suggested that I might have fallen off my bike. That would've been okay for people that didn't know me too well, but for anyone else I would have to think of something different, because they would probably know that I didn't have a bike.

I was kept off school for the week that followed. Dad went out every day saying he was looking for a job, and Kelly started to order me around the house from one chore to another and then back again. As I was running between jobs, she would often try to trip me up, or would follow me round shouting how I wasn't doing it right and needed to try harder.

When half term came round; Dad, Kelly and her three kids went away for a week to the coast. Somehow they had managed to talk Russell, who was still only about fourteen, into looking after Sarah and me while they were away. Personally I was over the moon that I wasn't going, but Sarah was a little upset. We had a good time with Russell and his girlfriend though, and really enjoyed ourselves.

As soon as Kelly got back after the holiday she went to check the larder. It was still well stocked but she wasn't happy about how much we had eaten while they were away. She took it out on Russell, accusing him of stealing all her kids' food for his girlfriend.

Russell argued back that he hadn't, and that he wouldn't see Sarah and me go without. The argument was still going on when Dad came in a few minutes later with the last of the bags from the car.

"This bastard has been stealing from us Jacob!" Kelly accused.

Dad didn't give Russell a chance to defend himself: he punched him in the face. The blow was so hard that Russell's feet came off the floor and he banged his head on the side before crumpling to the ground. Dad picked him up just to punch him back down.

When Russell tried to get up again, Dad knocked him

back down until Russell stopped trying. Then he grabbed him by the hair and dragged him down the hall and out the front door, slamming it shut after him. All the time the fight was going on, Sarah and me were trapped in the den screaming for them to stop.

Once Russell had been thrown out, Kelly insisted that all the food was to be locked away. Dad had quite a lot of odds and ends in the shed from various places or jobs, so he soon had a hasp and staple with a padlock in place. From now on, Kelly would ration the food and only cook for her kids, saying that I was old enough to fend for myself.

If I asked for food after that day I would be told I should've eaten at school and that that was enough for me. But if her own kids asked for an evening meal Kelly would throw tins of food at me with orders to feed them. Doing most of the cooking and all the washing up, I stopped asking, opting to eat scraps off the dirty dishes or out of the pans.

Life was becoming unbearable now; Dean would come up with stories about me and get me in trouble, sometimes telling several in the same day. These would nearly always mean I would get a few smacks, or sometimes the belt from Dad. Then if Kelly was in a good mood, I could go out once my chores were done, but with her bad days much more common, she would normally make me work until she went to bed.

In the mornings, I would find three portions of cereal with just enough milk so the other kids could eat. Then, after waking them for school, I'd watch them clean their bowls so as not to leave even a single cornflake for my breakfast. And after washing up I was off to school to be bullied for the day.

It must have been about six weeks after the fight with Russell that the social services turned up. We were all at school when they called at the house; I was late coming home that evening because of a detention. The other kids were in the den when I did get in, and I was surprised to see Kelly come out of there, followed a few seconds later by Dad.

"So we've been talking then, have we?" Kelly asked me.

"No," I replied.

"Well, why have we had the social here saying I don't feed you?" She kept calm, but the tone of her voice put the fear of God into me.

"I haven't said anything to anyone, honestly!" I replied, trying not to show how scared I was.

"What? So it must have been me telling them that, then? Is that what you're saying? Is it?" Kelly raised her voice with every word, shouting by the end.

"I don't know how they found out the larder is locked." I could hear the tremble of fear in my own voice as I answered.

"See Jacob, it was him!" she said, turning to Dad.

Dad walked up to me, –BANG! He gave me such a hard backhander that I was thrown halfway across the kitchen and into the cupboard doors.

"Who the fuck have you spoken to?" Dad demanded as he pulled me to my feet, –BANG! I didn't have time to answer before another backhander sent me to the other side of the room. He picked me up again and, –BANG! I'm off into the fridge before hitting the floor.

"You will fucking tell me boy! Who?" Dad may not have been shouting, but the way he said it I knew this wasn't finished yet, –BANG! I hit the fridge again.

I really don't know how many more times I was hit. I'm not even sure I was conscious after that one. The next vague memory I have, I was on the opposite side of the room from the fridge. I could make out voices and people's shapes, but not well enough to say who was saying or doing what for sure.

"Bring that shit here." Kelly I think. "This will make

him talk!"

Two people picked me up off the floor; Sarah told me later it was Kelly and Dean. I staggered a little but was more dragged in the direction of the cooker.

"Hold his arm." Kelly's voice for sure.

I was only semi-conscious but the heat from the gas flame was instant and unbearable. I managed to muster all my strength for one huge effort and got free. I stumbled backwards a step or two, and then my legs gave way, sending me into the cupboards once more.

"Leave him. He would have told us already, and besides, we don't really want to scar him, do we?" I passed out.

I don't know how long I lay there, it could have been hours. When I did come round, I was near the kitchen sink and it was dark. My head was killing me and I was unsteady when I eventually got to my feet. I stumbled, and fell back onto my hands and knees, before I crawled towards the stairs.

As I passed the living room door, it opened. "You're not going to school tomorrow," Dad calmly stated, and closed the door again.

I crawled up the stairs and into my room. Dean was already asleep on the bottom bunk, so when my first attempt to climb onto the top bunk failed, I just curled up where I had fallen and drifted off. The next morning I woke up to Dean kicking me in the head.

"I'm late, –where's my, –breakfast?" he shouted between kicks.

"He's not doing anything today!" Dad bellowed from his room. "Now go and pour your own bloody milk, you lazy bastard!" After one last kick, Dean left and I drifted off again.

It was well into the evening before I remember anything else. I was still curled up on my bedroom floor, then I noticed Sarah sitting in the doorway to my room.

"You okay?" she asked quietly.

Everything hurt and I was punch-drunk, but things were a little clearer. After a lot of effort, I managed to sit up and give her the best smile I could and nodded.

"Dad said you should have something to eat if you feel up to it," Sarah said, pushing a bowl of soup towards me.

"I'll try. How do I look?" I mumbled, taking a spoon though not really feeling up to eating.

"Bad. Do you want me to get a mirror?" She jumped up and headed for the bathroom, pausing when I said no, she came back with one anyway.

Both eyes were jet black and swollen almost shut; my nose was twice its normal size, looking more like a strawberry than a nose and my fat lips meant I couldn't close my mouth properly. Further down my body, it was hard to tell one bruise from another. So, from the waist up I was just a full rainbow of colours, along with dried blood covering my clothes.

I wished I hadn't taken the mirror now. I didn't just look bad, I looked like a heavyweight boxer's punch bag, and I didn't feel much different to one either. For the next few days I stayed in bed, only leaving my room to use the toilet or wash.

Then Kelly decided I was well enough to start my chores again. She would watch me every minute of the day, screaming for me to go faster. And when I still wasn't going fast enough for her, she took to kicking me instead. After about a week of this, Andy called for me to find out why he hadn't seen me at school. He knew I hated it there, but he knew I hated being at home more.

When he knocked I was ushered into the den at the back of the house, and Kelly rudely told him I had gone to my mum's and she didn't know if I was ever coming back.

Chapter 3

About a month later, Dean started playing up in the mornings, trying to get out of going to school. Sometimes he would sleep in, then say I didn't wake him. I got smacked for it a couple of times, but with Dad and Kelly sleeping in the next room I soon made sure they heard Dean get out of bed.

Other times he would take so long over breakfast he'd make both of us late for school. My punctuality record was already bad, so I'd get a letter to take home, then it was into the living room to drop my trousers and get my licks.

Dean's record was much better than mine so, it took a few weeks before he got his own letters about his attendance and punctuality. As it turned out, most of the time Dean was late, he hadn't gone to school at all.

After questions from his mum he blamed it on a bully in my year. It wasn't any of my doing – Steve also bullied me along with anyone else who wasn't strong or brave enough to fight back – but it still came down to me in Kelly's eyes.

After Dean's heart-to-heart with his mum, I got called into the living room. In the middle of the room was an upturned dining chair with its backrest lying on the floor.

Kelly instructed me on how to lie over the backrest and hold on to the legs, with my trousers and underwear round my ankles. Then Dad took his belt off and hit me twice before he shouted for me to go to my room.

As I stood up Kelly shouted, "Is that all this little shit gets for making my son terrified of going to school? Is it?"

"Get back down Dave." Dad bellowed, then he looked at me and pointed back to the chair.

As I got back into position, Kelly knelt down near my head and whispered, "This is going to hurt you a lot more than it will hurt me!" Then she poured the last of her drink over my bottom.

The drink wasn't hot, but with wet skin each of the next six lashes hurt at least twice as bad as the first two. But of course it didn't persuade Steve to stop bullying anyone. The next time Dean bunked off, Kelly went to the school to complain; that got Steve expelled.

Dean still bunked off school every now and again but now he got his own licks from his mum. She believed Dad didn't have the right to discipline her children, although it didn't stop her changing my normal punishment from a flat-handed smack to the belt over a chair. By now I was getting accused of so much I'd feel the belt two or three times a week.

After one of these belting sessions, when I took six of Dad's best for apparently swearing at Dean, I decided to run away. I went to Andy's first and asked his younger brother if I could borrow his bike for the day. He said okay, so long as Andy came with me, and together we rode in circles until I recognized Mum's flats.

No one was home when I knocked. Then as the minutes turned into hours I started to doubt whether we had even come to the right place, so I joined Andy when he turned for home. On the way back, he said he would have a word with his parents, and see if they could help me get in touch with my Mum.

I was still thinking this over as we headed in the general direction of home when something hard hit me on the back of the head. I looked over my shoulder just in time to get hit on the forehead by a second stone. We pedalled for all we were worth to get away from the older boys who were now using us as target practice. They got close a few times, but didn't hit either of us again before we were out of range.

"You had better get off home Dave," Andy said when we had slowed to a crawl to catch our breath.

We stopped so I could look in the mirror that Andy had attached to his bike. The right side of my face was dark red with blood flowing from a new gash on my forehead, the stone that hit the back of my head also left a nasty cut.

I really didn't want to go home. I knew Dad was out doing a job for a mate and Kelly couldn't drive, plus she probably wouldn't take me to hospital even if she could. So I suggested to Andy that we should turn towards his house.

Andy's mum, Rachael, was a nurse at the local hospital. So seeing blood still flowing freely when we arrived, she tried her best to stem the flow with a few butterfly stitches. That worked okay on my forehead, but with my hair in the way of the cut on the back of my head, I would need a hospital visit.

Rachael really wanted Dad to take me there, but after I explained that he was out working she took me herself. We weren't there very long and thankfully Rachael was never far away, which helped to keep my mind off having a total of seventeen stitches.

On our way back Rachael said she would need to see Dad because there was a letter from the hospital that he needed to read. So she asked the taxi driver to pass by my house, but when we came close I saw that Dad's car still wasn't there and we carried on back to hers.

When we got there she ran a bath for me. I wasn't allowed to wash my hair for a few days but, I cleaned most of the blood from everywhere else. Then Andy loaned me some clothes once I was dried off so mine could be washed, and Rachael cleaned my hair with something she had picked up at the hospital. Afterwards she insisted I ate something and took some painkillers for my headache.

Over dinner we talked about my plans for when I went home that evening, and I gave her the list of chores I knew would be waiting for me. Wash up, clean the kitchen, the den, bath and toilet, followed by hoover the hall, stairs and landing. Then, if I was lucky, I would be allowed to go to bed.

"They will make you do all that tonight?" Rachael asked when I finished.

"They would have me doing all that even if I was still bleeding," I said. Rachael smiled, thinking I was joking. As I smiled back I'm not too sure if I was; I had done a lot more in the past, feeling a lot worse than I did right then.

After dinner I sat on the couch and fell asleep. Rachael woke me shortly after eight o'clock to take me home. I asked for my clothes, but they were still in the wash and weren't dry yet. Andy told me the clothes I was wearing were a little small for him and said I could keep them if I wanted to, so after a drink we set off.

It was close to nine o'clock when we walked up the path to my house, making me about an hour late. Kelly answered the door when Rachael knocked on the front door.

"What's the little shit done this time?" Kelly asked abruptly.

"It's what's happened to him you should be asking. Now is Mr Baily there please?" Rachael didn't wait for an answer and pushed past Kelly, gently pulling me along beside her.

"Right you, off to bed and rest that head of yours," Rachael said, before gently kissing the uncut side of my head, as we reached the foot of the stairs. Then she turned and walked into the living room.

"Mr Baily? I'm sorry to barge in on you like this but Dave has just–," Kelly closed the door as she followed her in.

After all the riding about that day and a mild concussion, I was virtually asleep by the time Rachael came to my room a few minutes later to say goodnight. I remember her telling me, that she had ironed things out with Dad, and that I was to go to her house first thing in the morning so she could check on my stitches.

I got up early the following morning with a really bad headache. I wanted to get my chores done before Kelly woke up so was quickly dressed. A few minutes later, I was in the kitchen and saw my first chore of the morning, just about every piece of crockery we had was on the side needing to be washed up; that took a while to get done.

Afterwards I moved on to the den, and was tidying around when a knock at the door stopped me. We were not allowed to open the front door, unless we were told to, so I carried on cleaning the den quietly until Kelly answered it.

I recognised the man's voice straight away as Andy's dad, but he had kept his job as a police officer a secret, so I was a bit taken back when I saw him standing at the door in uniform.

"Hi Dave. I wanted to have a chat with you about what happened yesterday. Is that okay?" he asked as I came into view. I nodded it was.

"And I understand that Rachael wanted to see you today, so I thought I'd pick you up and have a chat with you and Andy together..., See if there's anything I can do for you. How's that sound?" he said, smiling politely.

"Yeah, that's okay..., sir," I answered, not knowing what to call him when he was in uniform.

"So if that's okay with you as well Mrs Baily, I'll take him off now?" he asked turning to Kelly.

Kelly turned to me before saying, "Well go on, if you're going, go. We don't want to keep the officer waiting," then turning back to Mr Frost she ruffled my hair and said, "and can you tell Rachael he was fine last night for me please." as charming as can be.

I was grinning from ear to ear as I left, not because Andy's dad had got me out of the rest of my chores, but because this was going to be my first ride in a police car. He even took a bit of a detour on the way when I asked if he could put the sirens on. When we did arrive at his house, he had to go off again straight away, but said he would be back later for that chat.

After saying hello to Rachael, she gave me a quick once over and was happy enough for me to play out, so long as I stayed close to the house with Andy. That was no hardship though: the garage was a playroom for Andy and his brother, and it was a lovely day on a quiet street, so with plenty to keep us occupied time flew past.

Before I knew it, Andy's dad came back with another officer for his lunch break. As the plates were cleared Andy's dad got back to work and talked about the stone-throwing the day before. He had previously arrested someone that fitted Andy's description of one of the guys, so he thought it might have been a revenge attack against him. Me being targeted was probably down to a case of mistaken identity or bad aim, with Andy the real target. This was one of the main reasons for him not wanting too many people knowing that he was with the police.

After our statements were taken, the second officer left. Then Andy was asked to occupy himself in the playroom for a bit, leaving his dad and me at the table.

"Don't worry about this guy, I'll find him and teach him not to throw stones at kids. I'm just sorry you got hurt so bad by some thug trying to get back at me. Now, is there anything else you would like to talk about Dave?" he said, smiling once we were alone.

"No..., Why?" I replied.

"Oh, it's just something that concerned Rachael last night. Did you mean what you said?" he asked, looking a little concerned.

"What about?" I answered, trying to think back.

"You know, about having to do all that work when you got in? Even if you were still bleeding?" he reminded me.

I had a little giggle. "No, I'm sure Dad would've taken me to hospital first."

He pinched my chin before asking, "How many children are there in the house?"

"There are five of us. My real sister and Kelly's three kids. Why?" I answered.

Mr Frost got up and headed across the kitchen to the fridge as he asked. "Do the others help with the chores?"

"Sometimes, if they're naughty." I told him.

"But you do most of them, is that right?" he continued, getting some juice.

"Yeah, I'm the oldest; it's my job to look after the others," I said, smiling broadly.

"Okay son, I'll leave it there for now. But if there's ever anything you ever want to talk about, you know you can tell me, don't let this uniform fool you..., I can keep a secret too you know." He winked before passing me the drinks to take to the playroom.

As he was leaving, he hugged Rachael and I overheard him say, "Maybe; see if he'll open up to you or Andy later."

I stayed with Andy in the playroom for the rest of the day. His mum would come in from time to time to see if we wanted anything, but nothing more, and all too soon it was time to say my goodbyes' and go home. When I got there, things carried on as normal, with Kelly immediately on my case to do the washing up, along with a load of other stuff she felt needed to be done, before I went to bed.

Andy started to ask me questions about my home life. Normally what I'd seen on TV or some other innocent question. But one morning when we met on the way to school I had a cotton wool patch over one eye.

"What happened to you last night then?" Andy said, pointing to the patch.

"Oh, nothing really, I just managed to burn myself with the chip pan," I replied casually.

"How did you manage that?" he asked, a little confused.

I explained that it was my own fault. Kelly had called for a takeout meal for herself and Dad, so it fell to me to cook for the kids. I was given a potato, a packet of bacon, a few eggs and some bread, so I made chips and grilled or fried the rest for everyone to make sandwiches. But when I put the chips in the hot fat, they were too wet, and, the pan splatted a glob of oil on me. Thankfully I had my eyes closed, because, it hit me just above my eye leaving a nasty blister.

"Mum was working last night, did you see her?" asked Andy once I'd finished.

"Na mate. Dad popped the blister. He said it will be fine in a few days," I answered, and waved the subject closed.

Andy pestered all that morning for me to see his mum so she could take a look at my eye. I agreed in the end, going to his place for lunch where I repeated my story to Rachael.

She looked at my eye and gave it a clean-up, saying that really Dad should have taken me to hospital straightaway. It was too late now to do anything more than keep it clean and hope for the best.

She gave me a couple of sterile wipes before I left with instructions on how and when I should use them. I did as she asked and cleaned my eye every morning and night until I ran out of wipes.

It was the weekend before I saw Rachael again and she quizzed me on my cooking. I found myself telling her that I only cooked once or twice a week, and that I enjoyed it. Most of the time it would just be something on toast anyway, so there wasn't much for me to hide, other than how often I was cooking.

In fact, at home during that time, if I was grounded or

off school for any reason, I would have to cook the other kids' dinner every night during the school week. Saturdays, I'd only cook if I were grounded, otherwise I was out all day. By the time I got in everyone would have eaten, and I wouldn't be allowed anything. On Sundays, Kelly would do a roast for her kids and Dad; I had to be in early to cook something for Sarah.

Rachael wasn't happy hearing that I wasn't supervised, but seemed to accept that I classed cooking as a treat, and then her questions turned to recipe suggestions. They sounded very nice, but I was unlikely to be given the ingredients to make beef stew and dumplings or spaghetti Bolognese.

On top of that during these days; three or four times a week I would be called into the living room to be accused of something. If I confessed to the crime, I was belted; if I denied it, I was shouted at, called a liar, and then belted. Sometimes I didn't bother saying anything, and just assumed my position over the waiting chair, and got belted.

Lying over the chair meant it was easier for Dad to hit me on the back of the legs rather than my bottom. Because this hurt one leg a little more than the other, I would end up with a limp for an hour or so after.

Then one morning before school, Dean was taking his time with breakfast, pushing the last spoonful around his bowl. He was actually off school that week because he had flu, and he'd already tried to make me late once. So I stood in the doorway of the den watching the minutes tick by on the clock, I stared at him.

"I'm already late so bloody hurry up will you?" I said abruptly. Dean just smiled back.

"Now or after school?" Dad said from behind me. I hadn't heard him come down the stairs.

I turned and walked to the living room taking my position over the chair. Dad gave me six of the best before I dressed myself, washed Dean's now empty bowl, and arrived at school five minutes late; getting me a week's detention and a bad report to take home. I was still limping when I took my seat next to Andy for an English lesson.

"Hurt your leg?" Andy asked as I pulled up my chair.

"It's nothing mate. Be alright in an hour or so," I answered, before the teacher gestured for us to be quiet. After the lesson, we sat on the field and continued chatting.

"How many?" Andy nodded at my legs.

"Three," I found myself saying.

"Belt?" he asked.

"Yeah. I swore at Dean this morning, Dad heard me," I told him, rubbing some life back into my sore leg.

"You've seen my dad's belt, haven't you?" Andy said, fixing his eyes on me.

"Yeah," I replied, looking back wide-eyed.

The belt had a thick brown leather strap and the buckle was a cowboy with a long bullwhip. It hung on the living room wall like an ornament. My own dad used the belt he wore every day, half the thickness and much more supple. I know which one I would prefer, I can tell you.

"He threatened me with that once, you know," Andy started to tell me. "Yeah. I started a fire in the garage with some oily rags. I almost burnt the whole house down, don't you know."

"What? Are you serious?" I was amazed at what I was hearing.

"Yeah, you want to know what my dad did to me?" he asked, nodding through the memory.

"Go on," I urged.

"He built the playroom so I wouldn't be bored." As Andy got up to leave, I looked up at him, speechless. "You should talk to him you know. My dad, he could help," he finished, offering me a hand up.

"No way! This is nothing to what would happen if they thought I had talked to…," I checked around as I got up, making sure no one was listening. "…the police. And I don't want you telling anyone either, right?"

"Okay," agreed Andy, after a short pause. "But if you don't want anyone else to find out you had better take these." He handed me a bag with a pair of tracksuit bottoms in it.

I hadn't told anyone about the beltings, and after the beating I took when the social had turned up, I had promised myself that I never would. But I hadn't thought that the strap marks on my legs could give the game away when I wore shorts during PE lessons. So I thanked Andy for the bottoms, and made him swear again not to tell anyone, before we went our separate ways.

Chapter 4

At the start of the summer break, the community youth club put on some activities for the local kids during the holidays. I had asked to go on a camping trip, but had done something or other wrong that had got me grounded, so I wasn't allowed. The other kids in the house did get to go, leaving me with all the chores. With them done, I'd normally sit in my room, reading or trying to catch up on my schoolwork.

A few days into the holidays, Kelly thought I wasn't doing enough saying that I should do some washing. Thinking she meant the dishes, I went to the kitchen, but it was spotless. Moments later, she called me back upstairs, where I found all my clothes in a bath of water.

My clothes weren't in great condition, but I took my time and did the best job I could at washing them. A few hours later, with everything on the line outside to dry, I was called back to the living room for more instructions and told to clean the bath. It only took a few minutes, but when I got back downstairs, after another shout from Kelly, I found all my clothes on the kitchen floor.

"Fell off the line didn't they. Do 'em again!" was Kelly's next order. This went on for the rest of the day and well into the night.

Each time I hung my clothes out to dry, Kelly would rip them off the line for me to do again. In the end, everything was in a worse state than when I started. The next day it was Dean's bedding that I had to wash time and time again. After a couple of days of this, Andy came to knock for me with his mum.

"See mum, he is here." I heard the voice of my best mate, as I walked past the open front door.

"Shall we give these two five minutes and have a quick chat Mrs Baily?" Rachael asked politely. Kelly invited her in and left Andy and me to go into the garden.

Sitting on the front lawn Andy told me about a treehouse he planned to build during the holidays, and asked for my help. I said no, knowing I wouldn't be allowed to because of my grounding. Then Rachael came back out and it was time to say my goodbyes'.

"No, you're coming too," Rachael said in reply to my wave. "You're still grounded mind, so I'll be keeping a close eye on you."

"Okay," I replied joyfully, knowing that there would be no more chores for a few hours.

Over the next week or so I had to be in by five, and then I was set to work by Kelly, but the rest of the day I spent with Andy and his father working on the treehouse.

As the week passed, the treehouse build went well, and we finished well ahead of schedule. Then the night it was completed, Andy and I insisted on sleeping in there. Rachael cleared it with Dad for me to stop over for the night, so we bedded down and made plans to spend the rest of the holidays camped in Andy's back garden.

During my daily visits, his mum would often pull me to one side and chat about how things were at home. I had begun to trust her, so I said how I always seemed to be in trouble for one thing or another, and that Kelly's kids were always believed over me.

Andy's parents had already started planning a fishing trip at a local camping site for the following week. They asked if I'd like to go but I turned them down, not really wanting to leave Sarah alone when she got back from her own trip.

Andy's parents were very insistent though, and I eventually asked Dad. He said no at first, then Andy's dad came round to have a word with him. After he told Dad that he runs a strict household, and, I'd be treated no different to his own children, he changed his mind.

The night before I was due to leave, Kelly checked

what I had packed to take with me. Most of my clothes were ruined when she had me washing them all day, so she repacked my bag with Dean's clothes. Then she warned me that if anything happened to them that I'd be 'in for it' when I got back.

The holiday was fantastic, with fishing the main focus, and on the first full day I caught a whopper. The problem was I had never fished before and didn't have a clue what to do. Worse still, Andy's dad was away getting some drinks so, I started panicking that the fish would die if I didn't get the hook out pretty damn quick.

I grabbed some forceps out of the box and got the hook free without really thinking, then I watched as the fish swam away, alive and well. Suddenly, I felt exhausted, and fell back.

"You can put the maggot on for me!" I said to Andy, and started to laugh my head off.

Andy's dad had seen everything on his way back, and congratulated me on getting the fish away alive. He asked where I had learned to do that, and was surprised to hear that I'd never fished before, with me saying, "It seemed the right thing to do." When we got back to the chalet later that night my fish was still the talk of the day, it was the biggest catch too.

So with the day coming to an end, Andy and I were on the floor play fighting when Rachael said she had another surprise for me. I was asked to open my wardrobe: and when I did I found that all the clothes I'd brought with me had been replaced with brand new ones.

I was overjoyed, and we had a fantastic time, with long days of fishing and local attractions. We also had long nights talking about my home life. I had a great deal of trust in Andy's parents now, so I told them everything that was going on, holding little back.

During one of these tearful evening talks, they said about the social and how they could help me. They asked me to talk to someone while we were still away, but I told them how scared I was of Dad finding out. Besides, I wanted Sarah to be with me every step of the way, because given the pattern so far, either her or Dean, was going to be the next victim if I left them alone.

Rachael explained that they could still help by giving me a safe place to see someone – Sarah too, if I could manage to get her out for a few hours. They didn't push me into anything, so I said I'd think about it, and we got on enjoying the rest of our time away.

On the last day of the holiday I asked for my clothes back. When Rachael told me she had thrown them out by mistake I went weak at the knees and fainted.

Once I'd recovered, I told her that the clothes weren't mine, and the warning I had been given if anything happened to them. Rachael phoned Dad and explained her mistake and how bad she felt, adding she would take Dean shopping for some new clothes when we got back. Then I spoke to Dad and he assured me that I wasn't in any trouble, which helped make me feel a little better, so I cheered up a little.

When we arrived back at Andy's house I got very upset again, knowing that I was probably going back home to the belt and questions about what I had said during the holiday. Andy must have seen how upset I was, and brought me his dad's belt.

Taking it from him, I turned it over in my hands, feeling the weight of the metal buckle and the stiffness of new leather, thinking how much more this belt would hurt than my own dad's.

"He's never used it you know," Andy said, looking at me. I stared back at him confused, as he continued. "It was a leaving present from his last station. You shouldn't be belted Dave, you're not a bad boy you know." I cried, and agreed to speak to someone.

His parents arranged for me to see a friend of theirs

who had helped with the fostering of Andy's brother, another well-kept secret until then.

Erin was a lovely woman with a caring attitude, and had become a personal friend to the family. She would come round regularly in the evenings now and chat with me, and I eventually opened up to her after several weeks of visits.

One day, when I got six from the belt for getting a detention at school, we talked about the levels of punishment I was receiving and why I hadn't spoken before. I told her it was all to protect Sarah, and was scared that if I told people I'd be taken away, then Dad would start belting her next. I had seen it with Russell and Adrian, so to me it was logical.

Erin offered to help, saying she could get me out straightaway, although for Sarah it would be different. With no evidence that she had ever been mistreated, Sarah's case would need to be investigated first.

My own investigation had taken months, in Sarah's case it could take even longer, unless she got hit. But there might be a way if Erin could get a statement from one of the other kids in the house, about seeing what I was going through.

By now it was early November, and in the fine autumn evenings the local kids, including myself, were making a bonfire ready for Guy Fawkes' Night. One evening I got called back to Andy's house to have a word with his parents.

"Look son, I've been talking it over with Erin, and…, me and Rachael, well, we've got an idea, okay?" Andy's dad started as I took a seat at the table. "Andy tells me it's your sister's birthday soon. Well, what about having a party for her here. We'll invite Erin along and see what we can do from there? How's that sound?" he finished.

I was smiling away, so he knew I'd agreed.

"Not done yet tyke," he said, stopping me jumping

round the kitchen. "I also wanted to ask you how you'd feel about staying with us after all this is over."

I was a little confused and stared at him for a moment.

"We're going to ask to foster you; if that's okay with you of course." Mr Frost asked. He just about finished speaking before I knocked him off the chair jumping up to hug him.

It couldn't be simpler really. Erin would become Sarah's social worker, with her evidence coming out of the party; any problems from Dad, and Mr Frost would have him arrested within minutes.

Then with my case being so violent, Sarah and I would both be put into protective care, and from there we would have been put up for fostering. The Frosts, having fostered before, just needed to put some paperwork through the system, and Erin would make sure I was offered them as first choice of placement.

Sarah wouldn't be able to join me because of the lack of room in the house, but she would be kept as close as possible. And because Andy's dad was a police officer, I would get open access to see her, even if I needed him to escort me.

Overjoyed, there now came the saddest day of my life.

It was November, the night of the fourth. Andy had been guarding the local bonfire because some thugs had threatened to set it alight the night before it was due. He was with a neighbour and his son – I'm afraid I don't remember their names, or I would certainly mention them. It is believed they dozed off, having taken shelter too close to the bonfire when a couple of drunks walked past and set it alight for a laugh.

Then news came; Mr Frost had crashed his panda car when he heard over the radio – his son, my best mate, had been identified as one of the victims of the fire. We were told Mr Frost died on impact and didn't suffer, and I take solace in that.

Also that night, Mrs Frost was first on the scene of the fire, living just a hundred metres away. There she was witness to her only natural born son's death as she continued in vain to help the injured.

We had arranged for Erin to come to Sarah's eighth birthday party the following Saturday, less than four days away. I have never spoken of this before writing this book, but I wish them all peace wherever they may be. I loved you all as if you were my own and have missed you ever since. xXx

Do you remember my childhood years?

With summertime holidays and cold ice cream ears.

The glint of sunshine on our hair,

as we stood watching the summer fair.

The coconut shies and lucky picks,

our sticky fingers in candy floss dips.

The flashing lights and thumping beat,

our tired eyes, our aching feet.

Our worn-out legs so tired and heavy,

your Daddy's arms so strong and steady.

He held me close, his voice still clear,

his soothing words ringing in my ear.

I placed my head upon his chest,

his cuddles were warm and always the best.

This memory I have, so strong and clear,

my lasting memory, of a yesteryear.

Chapter 5
Life Without . . . the Frost's
It is here that my story begins.

And so we continue with the sad times. Obviously, all talk went straight to the accident and the funerals, which I had little or no involvement in, so it took a few days before Rachael sat me down with Erin.

"We still want to help you Dave, but I think you know that with what's going on right now..., we..., I mean...," Erin stuttered to a stop and we all sat with a tear in our eye. "I still want to move forward with your case as soon as we can, okay?" she continued after a few moments.

"What about Sarah?" I asked.

"Well, the thing is Dave, without a safe house for her I would have no option but to let your father take her home. And with what we have so far I wouldn't be able to get anyone assigned to her until there has been an investigation carried out. You know there's no other way now, don't you?" Erin replied, dejected that she couldn't do more.

"Then I'll say that I was lying about everything and stay with Sarah until we find another way. Okay?" I insisted.

"But—," Erin started, before Rachael's crying stopped her.

"It's okay Rachael, I understand," I said, knowing she couldn't help me, not right now anyway.

As I hugged Rachael she said, "I'm putting your name on the headstone Dave. He would have been proud of you."

"But Dad's going to pick me up! What if he sees it?" I looked at her before sobbing, "Had better not."

"Dave, the press are going to be there, and if they

ever get hold of you and your story you won't need to worry about your dad anymore." Rachael was saying as she took hold of my hands. "So it's going on there, right?" she finished, not doing a very good job of looking angry. I let her win with a big hug.

A few days later we had the joint funeral. I was so upset that I didn't go to the ceremony itself, but Erin stayed with me for comfort, and a couple of days after that I said my final farewell to Rachael and the rest of the family.

Erin said she would stay in touch, but I lost the number she gave me. There was no other way for us to talk without Dad finding out, so I never heard from her again either.

I don't really remember the first few weeks after the funeral, but I know I cried a lot. People came to talk to me and I hardly noticed they were there, and then they would go again. I eventually withdrew from everyone, staying in my room nearly all the time.

I know that Dad got advised to move me away from the area to help with my recovery. He put in for various transfers but got refused due to rent arrears, which would take some time to be cleared up.

Somehow, crying, alone in my room, I could still do wrong in Kelly's eyes. I was too loud or could even be too quiet, though normally I was too lazy to get out of bed. She would shout her head off for a few minutes to get Dad's attention. He would then have a few minutes' shouting himself, before giving me a few smacks. I could tell he was holding back though, because they really didn't hurt.

When I went back to school, I became a loner, hiding away from comments about the accident. Then I started to avoid doing sports and get away from the bullies for a while. Everyone was better than me anyway so, when teams were picked, I'd be the one that no one wanted on their side. The one exception to this was swimming.

Even though I couldn't swim, I still enjoyed going. After changing into trunks I'd be sent to the shallow end of the pool, with fewer of the other kids joining me each week. There the lifeguard would let us play for a little while before going through some confidence-building exercises. Then at the end of each lesson, the pool would be marked out for various swimming tests.

That part I hated, and I would try to get to the changing room before anyone noticed. More often than not I got caught, so I would have to jump in the pool to splash about until I got a mouthful of water, panic, and fail my test, if I didn't need to be rescued.

About six months before I was due to move up to senior school, I was the only non-swimmer left in my year, and the jeering from the other kids had me crying at the side of the pool. Lilly-Ann, one of the girls in my class came over and asked me why I couldn't swim just fifteen metres. My crying just got worse so she got a lifeguard to come over. He sat down and comforted me until all the other kids had gone to get changed.

"Try it now that there's no one else here," Lilly-Ann suggested, and with a reassuring nudge from the lifeguard, I jumped back in the pool.

The test started the same as all the others, and less than halfway across the pool I panicked. I was making so little headway that even the pole to drag me to safety, just six inches away, looked like it was a mile. My head started bobbing under the surface every few seconds, and I heard Lilly-Ann shout that she wouldn't like me if I failed again; then the lifeguard dived in.

I relaxed and went under, then kicked and broke the surface again. The lifeguard was still a few feet away but he didn't seem to be getting any closer. I kept on kicking and moving my arms, hoping he wouldn't take much longer to get to me, but he stayed just out of reach.

"We don't teach you to tread water until Level Three

you know. Now, how about we try getting to the side first eh' chap?" he said, nodding towards the side.

I made a lunge for him, with pleas' that I couldn't swim, and he backed away. I lunged again and he backed off some more. Each time I made a move for him, he would move back about the same amount. Then, with Lilly-Ann screaming, "You're doing it!" I realised I wasn't going under anymore.

It took some minutes to reach the other side, and a few more before I could pull myself out of the pool, but I had passed basic swimming. With newfound confidence, a few weeks later I went on to pass my Level One test, and then there was no stopping me.

When I moved up to senior school a few months later, things at home changed. Dean would still say that I did something or other that should have got me belted, but Dad wouldn't believe him because I was in a different school now.

Kelly's chore list never let up, though now between jobs I had to stand on the bottom step so she could see me from the living room. Every now and then she would push past me to go upstairs for 'something she'd forgotten'. On the way back down she would push me off the step again.

Around the school, some of the kids who had also known the Frost family started to taunt me over their deaths, causing me to become very withdrawn again. This went on for weeks before one lad really got to me. He had followed me for days with nothing good to say before I decided to meet him for a chat.

Jason was in the year above me, and was a lot bigger. I wouldn't have called him a bully as such; he was just showing bravado in front of even bigger lads than himself. I was a good target, being a skinny eleven-year old.

That day, I skipped my last lesson and hid behind the

gate waiting for Jason to leave school. As he walked past, I jumped from my hiding place, and grabbing the strap of his bag, dragged him to the ground.

I tried to punch him in the face, but he got hold of both my hands and we rolled about, wrestling each other. A few minutes later, the crowd were saying a teacher was on his way, so everyone scattered.

I knew where Jason lived, so I ran as fast as I could to the route he would be taking home. All the kids that had seen our first encounter seemed to be with him, but I still managed to run through the crowd and surprise him again.

Jumping on his back, I sent him headlong to the ground. He squirmed about but I managed to get a few punches in before he made it back onto his feet. Once we were both up, we punched, kicked and bit each other until we fell over again. Then back on the ground, Jason held up his hands to surrender.

As I got up the crowd parted for me to go, and leaving Jason on the floor to catch his breath, I walked off in the direction of home. Then the crowd turned their attention on Jason, calling him a wimp for not being able to beat up a first-year student.

Because of all the shouting, I didn't hear Jason run up behind me. He barged me to the ground and as I rolled over he jumped on top of me. I took a few good punches to the head before I got free.

Once I was loose though, I got him in a headlock, and after turning him over, gave him some of his own medicine, punching him in the face a few times. About then, Russell walked past and shouted, "Need any help Dave?"

"I'll take care of my own problems, thanks!" I called back, still punching.

After screaming at Jason how to speak about my friends in future, and with another punch or two to demonstrate my point, the fight was over.

The following day I was sent to see the headmaster as soon as I got to school. He asked why I started the fight, so I told him some of the things Jason had been saying to me over the past few days. He caned me twice before calling Jason in. He got two strikes as well, for fighting a smaller boy.

That helped, and the bullies backed off for a while. And I would never hear another bad word said about the Frost's after that day, either.

After being withdrawn for so long, it was good to have won a friend during my fight. Ron it turned out, shared most of my classes, but I remember him most as having a love for acting, which will come into focus very soon. He didn't live far from school, so I'd walk him home every day, and it wasn't long before we became close friends.

It was still fairly early in the school year when a drama company came to my school. They wanted to do a project with some first-year students, and so each class was called on stage for an audition. We didn't have to do a play, just some exercises in mime: to show you were happy you'd walk about with a smile; to show excitement you'd jump about doing whatever.

Then we were asked to show sadness, and on command I burst into floods of tears. My drama teacher was surprised that I was really crying, and came over to comfort me. I had learnt by then how to bury my feelings deep inside, so I quickly returned to my usual self. My class was picked for the project and my drama teacher later told me that I was the main reason for her choice.

We started the project and over the coming weeks it all came together. We were going to do a mime about a hunter-gatherer tribe from the Stone Age. I would play joint lead, with Ron winning the other lead role.

The play started with Ron and I showing our real

friendship on stage as we jointly led the tribe. Then, during some lean times we argued over leadership, splitting the tribe in half.

I left for pastures new with half the tribe, but it wasn't long before we realised we had too little grain to last the winter. I decide to lead a small party back, asking for help, though my intention was mistaken: so Ron, thinking I had come with a war party, challenged me to a fight.

I held my hands up to show that I was there in peace but was killed, more by accident than a result of any fight, banging my head on a rock. My real intentions then came out and the tribe becomes reunited again. At the end members of both sides of the tribe lifted me up in honour as the curtain came down.

We tried to show that it was better to listen to others before you judged them, and though the price I paid was high, it was a valuable lesson for the tribe to learn.

We rehearsed for weeks, and when we got it about right we played in front of the other first-year students. After the performance we got in position and took our final bow in front of at least a hundred silent faces. We left the stage feeling as dejected as eleven-year olds could, with heads bowed.

"AGAIN!" a kid shouted from the hall.

"MORE!" another kid shouted, and then the clapping started.

As we took the stage for a second time the whole audience rose to their feet. The noise became deafening to the point where we couldn't hear our names being called back stage. The headmaster had watched the show, of course, and seeing this reaction he wanted us to perform for the whole school.

We performed every day the following week, once for each year, ending on Friday with an evening performance. To this one the parents and anyone else who wanted to see it again could come. So many people wanted to watch the show, the school ended up arranging for a local theatre to let us perform there during the first week of the coming holidays.

There were still a few weeks to go before that, so costumes were improved and we made a few bits of scenery. To keep in practice we would perform at the junior schools in the local area. That way, any younger kids who couldn't go to the upcoming evening performances would get a chance to see the show.

Life was good then. Dad had gone to the first evening performance and loved the show. Kelly would still try to get him to hit me for one reason or another, but Dad rarely did anything.

Then Kelly started to push me into doors and walls around the house. That calmed down after I brought my costume home and changed it from a tunic to a loincloth. After that, if I did anything wrong, which was often in Kelly's eyes, I would end up locked in my room between chores.

There were six shows put on during the holidays, each receiving a standing ovation from the capacity crowd. Then we were told a TV crew were going to record our last performance for the local evening news. So, with reporters hanging around everywhere, I asked if I was likely to be interviewed.

"What?" my drama teacher said, sounding surprised. "A rags to riches case like you? I want to read about how you got here after…," As she stuttered to a stop, I knew she was talking about Andy's death. She had taken me to the cemetery a few weeks before and asked what his brother was like.

"I'm going to make damn sure they don't miss you out this time Dave. Now go on, this is your five-minute call." She finished after a few moments. I smiled as I ran off and got ready to perform.

After the play ended, I was asked to hang about

because there was a reporter who wanted to interview me at Andy's grave side. Then he was going to do a story showing how I had coped with the depression of his death, just a year before, so well with acting.

I thought they meant for me to wait where I was, so I stayed near the stage door long after the crowd of kids getting autographs had gone. When my drama teacher found me, she said that the reporter had been looking for me but had to go to make his deadline. It's a pity, because if they had asked about the headstone, which reads…

✠

ANDY & ANDY
FROST
**A FATHER MUST GUIDE HIS SON
TO HIS SEAT NEXT TO GOD
AND TOGETHER THEY WILL REST
REMEMBERED BY THE MANY
THEY LEAVE BEHIND**

RACHAEL
AN EVER LOVING MOTHER A PRECIOUS WIFE

...

DAVE
**THE BRAVE SON AND DEVOTED BROTHER
THEY WANTED SO MUCH**

…they would have had a different story that day. And so, maybe, would I.

Chapter 6

During the holidays, the transfer for the house came through and we moved to a different part of town, so naturally I'd be starting at a new school. The headmaster there asked to have a meeting before I started, and talk about my up and down behaviour. My old drama teacher had also been asked to visit, and so along with Dad they talked about my school reports.

My punctuality was appalling; I don't remember a single week in which I wasn't late for school at least once, so I was always in detention. I'd also been caned about a dozen times for fighting; not that I started them anymore; I just got caught a lot after the bullies had run off.

They ummed and ahhed their way through the meeting, saying that I now had a fresh start, and to help push me in the right direction they wanted to show the play, and introduce me to the school that way. I begged them not to, knowing it would only point me out to the bullies as a sissy actor, but they made the arrangements anyway.

So it was decided that we would perform the play on the first day after the holiday, but only about half the cast turned up. We had a quick change-about with parts to fit the numbers and performed anyway. After the final bow, the headmaster called for me to join him on the stage.

"This is Dave Baily. He will be staying with us now, so if anyone wants to know how to become a budding actor like this boy, just ask him," the head announced to the assembled kids as I came to his side.

It took about an hour for Tony to find me; he wanted to know how much lunch money I had, so I told him, we were on free meals and I didn't have any. He didn't like that, of course, but he still invited me to meet him after school to show me around the estate.

Tony was a lot bigger than me, so I knew what was going on straightaway, but I said I would meet him anyway and thought about whether to get put on report on my first day.

At the time I stood a proud four-foot-six, and came in a little over four stone, but I thought I had a chance. After all, I had taken the punches of my eighteen-stone Dad, so, what was this kid really going to do to me? And I had learnt by then that I didn't need to win anyway, I just needed to fight, and then he would go elsewhere for an easier time.

Tony was at the school gates as planned, and we walked around chatting for about half an hour. As we went, he showed me where the park was, and a couple of places where the local kids would meet up after school. It was going great until he offered to buy me a drink. On the way to the shops we walked down an alley and met five of his mates. I didn't stand a chance.

Two of them pinned me against the wall and they took it in turns punching me in the head and chest. Then, after going through my pockets and still finding no lunch money, they started again. I saw one punch coming and managed to move my head out the way, so, the lad punched the wall instead. Another lad kicked me in the groin, sending me to the ground in agony.

They carried on for a few minutes, kicking me while I was on the ground, but I was so tightly balled up I hardly felt them. Then I caught one of their legs and bit into the lad's calf.

"I'm going to make you look so bad your mother won't recognise you!" he sneered down, before between them, they wrestled off my clothes and trainers, ripping them to rags as they ran off.

The smirk on Kelly's face, Dad smiling as he stood behind her, when I walked into the kitchen; beaten black and blue from head to toe, bleeding, standing in only my underpants and socks, aged about eleven.

"So what have we done this time, *BOY?*" Kelly growled. I saw the hatred in my step mothers' eyes; she had recognised me!

Dad would only hit me if he thought I'd done something wrong, and he could see that I'd basically been mugged. He looked me up and down, grunted, and went into the living room.

Then Kelly came over and, grabbing a handful of hair, she dragged me up the stairs, shouting that I had no respect for the things she bought for me. When we got to my room she threw me towards the bed; I twisted my body so managed to land sitting on the mattress. She followed me in, and grabbing some more hair, threw me into the pillow as hard as she could.

"Can't you fucking sit still while I shout at you?" she screeched in my ear. As I sat up, she threw me down again.

Before I could sit up again she jumped on top of me, pinning me to the bed with her knees. She screamed down that she was going to kill me if I didn't get her clothes back, while slapping my face as hard as she could. I cried back that she would go to jail for murder, but she shouted that she'd get off with manslaughter, and when she got out it would be Sarah's turn.

Then snatching the pillow from under my head she forced it into my face. I was fighting for all I was worth to get free but, after she punched me in the belly, I couldn't get a breath. Then everything seemed to become calm and silent.

I must have passed out because, when I opened my eyes' Dad was sitting on my bed, trying to comfort me. He was telling me that everything was going to be okay, saying Kelly was just wound up after a stressful day, so, she didn't really mean anything she'd said. Then after saying "Sorry", he fixed a padlock to my door and locked me in.

So on my first day of school I got to meet the six biggest bullies on offer. Beaten black and blue or not, the following morning I was going to be caned and classed as a troublemaker. And the way Kelly acted after! I wasn't stupid; I was fucked. And Kelly had made sure that I knew it.

The place:
A four-bedroom house in the centre of a council estate; a mid-terrace, it had the living room at the back, where Kelly would hide if someone knocked, along with the kitchen. I didn't walk out of these two rooms as often as I walked into them. Also there was another room at the front, along with a toilet at the bottom of the stairs.

Upstairs; my sparsely furnished bedroom overlooked the street at the front of the house. Dad and Kelly slept opposite at the rear. There were also the other two smaller bedrooms, one front one rear, and the family bathroom. The other kids changed rooms at Kelly's whim, often in the middle of the night, so, I never did keep up with who was where.

Every door in the house had a hasp and staple fitted within days of us arriving. Every kitchen cupboard and drawer was padlocked shut from the first day; and high hedges surrounded the large gardens front and rear.

The punishments:
The cane was the worst of my regular punishments, a metre and a half section of an old fishing rod. Dad had stripped everything off, leaving what looked, and felt, like a nylon whip. As it cut through the air it made a high-pitched whistle, and I knew when it stopped, it was going to *HURT*!

It left a thin red line, looking and feeling like a burn at first, although by morning each one would be two inches wide. Sometimes, I would have to get Sarah to count them while they were fresh or they would blend into one big blister. Then as they healed, they would weep constantly, making my trousers stick to the back of my legs. The pain from pulling them up or down was sometimes as bad as the caning itself.

The belt was easy until part of the backrest of the chair broke. Dad took the rest out and started using the buckle end of his belt. From then on he would get it to wrap around my legs and hit me in my well-placed and now unprotected groin.

Grounding meant I was locked in my room, more often than not with Dean. He would be told to torment me until I started a fight, then Dad would cane me for it, while Dean and Kelly watched.

When I did make it out of my room if I came within striking distance of Kelly or Dean, a punch or a kick would come my way. If I fought back or tried to defend myself, Dad caned me.

The windows will soon be screwed shut, with boards stored in the next room, in case I smashed the glass. And I never had a light bulb, just in case I decided to hurt myself.

The main excuses:

Kelly loved recounting her days as a leader in the Girl Guides, saying how she had dealt with difficult children and had enjoyed the challenge. Then if I had any visible bruising, which was most of the time, she'd say I'd been fighting with Dean or at school, which would also explain the cane marks. Sometimes, she would also tell people I had become very accident prone, and often sleepwalked, falling down the stairs in the middle of the night.

When I asked if it was okay to lock me in my room, Dad told a social worker he only locked the doors when the house was empty in case there was a break-in. That way the thief would only be able to get into one room. As for the discipline, Dad apparently left that to Kelly, thinking he might hurt a child a little too much if he smacked us himself.

In the house:

Dean, Kelly's eldest. He was three months younger than me and jealous I would leave school a year before him. Bigger than me, but not by much, he was the bully I couldn't get rid of. Daily he would come home with stories about what I had done wrong, most of them untrue, and then watch as I was punished.

Suzanne was around the same age as Sarah and shared most of her classes at school. She was an angel in her mum's eyes – the devil's advocate in everyone else's. Even back then, she was a spiteful bitch, wanting everything her way. If she didn't get it, it would be taken out on me.

Dad was a lazy fat bastard who always wanted to please his wife, and answer her every whim to get an easy life. Nearly six foot tall and eighteen stone with greasy black hair. He hadn't had a job for the past three years because he thought the dole paid enough. His one good point was that he would give a reason for hitting me – maybe not a good reason, but a reason nonetheless.

Kelly, or 'The Bitch', as she would later have us all call her, was exactly that. Very charming and polite when we had visitors, behind closed doors she constantly screamed at someone. Average build and looks for a woman her age, she didn't need reasons to hit anyone.

Once she called me to her because she was bored. Grabbing my ears she banged my head against the wall to the beat of 'I Want to Break Free'. After the song finished, she told Dean to carry on. It took two more tracks before I was lying unconscious on the floor.

Sarah, my little sister, who had to hide away to study. She cried often having to tell on me for something I hadn't done, for fear of being hurt by Suzanne. Along with the other kids she was forced to watch some of the events in this book, with a warning that she would get the same if anyone knew about it.

And me?

Fucked is an understatement. I would have probably been dead within a week if I hadn't of done something.

In reality, I didn't have a cluc what to do except get out of the house – fast. Just seconds after the lock on my door snapped shut, I jumped out of the window and ran up the road, still only in my underwear.

I didn't know where I was, or where to go, so I hid behind a wall to try and think of somewhere I could get help. About twenty minutes later a police officer found me there shivering.

On the short walk back to the house he asked what had happened to me. I told him about my walk with Tony, and then went through what happened when I got home. He reckoned I must have fallen asleep and had a bad dream or something, because no parent would act like that after their kid had just been beaten up.

When we got to the house Dad was in the front garden. He claimed that he'd just finished cleaning the windows, explaining the ladders that he had with him. A minute or so later Kelly joined us.

"Oh this boy," she said to the officer politely while she hugged Dad. "He's always getting up to stuff like this to get attention. He's jealous of his younger brother you see. We've got a meeting about it at the school tomorrow. Don't worry, we'll take care of him now and make sure he doesn't bother anyone else tonight."

They chatted for a few moments until the officer was satisfied. Then he said his goodbyes' and left us at the top of the garden path.

Kelly put her hand on my shoulder and gently led me to the house and through the front door. As soon as the door closed her manner changed. She grabbed me by the hair again and dragged me up the stairs, throwing me into my room.

"Try something like that again and you'll never leave this room alive," she snarled and slammed the door shut.

A short time later a bucket was thrown in with me and the door was locked. I found some clothes and tried the window, but it wouldn't open, so I crawled under my bed, shaking with fear, hoping she wouldn't come back.

The following morning, Kelly dragged me from under the bed and took me to school. I hardly got a word in as she explained to the headmaster that I was always starting fights and then claiming I was beaten at home.

After she had added that the social services had a file on me, and with my past school reports in front of him seeming to backup Kelly's story, the headmaster decided to cane me.

Now I really knew I was in big trouble: with caning on the list of punishments I could get at home without it being noticed too much. I had to talk to someone soon without Kelly getting in the way.

I started swearing at the headmaster and calling him a wimp until he caned me again. Then I screamed at him to go and get my little sister because she could do a better job. That got me two more, but it had the desired effect. Though it left me with a two-week suspension that I didn't really want, it also meant that the social would be visiting me the following morning.

The rest of that week would see a social worker coming round to the house in the morning and spending an hour or so with Kelly and Dad, chatting. Then I'd be called to the living room and asked to explain why I insisted on telling such lies to cover up my bad behaviour.

It shocked Kelly when I asked to see Erin, but the social worker came back the next day saying that she no longer worked for them. Apparently she had no open cases when she left, and he couldn't find any records about me.

"You'd better fuck off and look again then hadn't you," I said when he'd finished explaining. I carried on swearing at the worker until he did leave.

Then Kelly dragged me upstairs with the schoolwork that he'd dropped off, and locked me in my room. She went out shortly after that, but not before putting a speaker next to my door and filling the room with white noise. Sometime later I was let out to cook dinner for the kids.

My last meeting with the social that week, he just opened my door to say goodbye. Kelly locked it after he left and it wasn't opened again till the following morning.

"Out!" Kelly screamed as my door swung open the following Saturday. Sarah had gone to visit Mum that weekend, but I hadn't been allowed to go because of my suspension. So with really nothing to do in a new area except get beaten up, I stayed on the bed reading, not really interested, and feeling I might even be safer locked in my room.

"Fucking get out now, you little shit!" Kelly screamed, snatching my book and throwing it out the door. Then she hit me in the belly, dragged me downstairs, and out the front door with instructions to be back in by six.

I hung around near the house for a little while, getting my bearings, until Dean was told to chase me off. Then I ambled around the estate for a bit. Other than a day at school, this was my first time out of the house alone since arriving, and I didn't know what else to do.

I got back home I thought in plenty of time, but I was twenty minutes late. Dad gave me a quick backhander and sent me to my room. When I got there I found Dean had moved in with a little furniture. Now there were two single beds, a small wardrobe and a dining chair. As I went into my room Dean smiled across at me.

"I've left you a present, hope you like it," he said, nodding in the direction of my bed.

When I sat on my mattress I found that it was soaked, so I jumped across the room and punched Dean in the face. Seconds later, Kelly opened the door and pulled me off him by my hair. Dad followed her in and I was caned six times over the chair. Once he'd finished, Kelly screamed in my ear, "You two had better start getting on because you're spending the next week together."

As soon as Dad and Kelly left the room, Dean was instantly on my case again, bringing Dad back to add two more licks to shut me up. I tried to stay out of Dean's way after that and not rise to his taunts. Later that evening, he told me he was getting paid ten pence from his mum for every lash I took, and that he wanted a Walkman, so he was going to make sure I took a lot.

I waited well into the night before I jumped on top of Dean, letting him know I could hurt him before his mother could come to the rescue. He got the idea, taking a bloody nose. Kelly came in then to drag me off him, breaking my nose with a karate chop.

That night, Dean went back to his own room. He didn't try anything when I saw him the following night, but he told me the social weren't coming back because they thought my behaviour had improved enough.

Dean still went to school during the second week of my suspension, leaving me at home alone with Kelly. I don't know where Dad was going; he left early and came back after dark. So for the rest of that week, Kelly had me running around the house doing her endless chores.

If I wasn't doing anything I had to stand at the bottom of the stairs and wait for her to think of something. Whenever she passed me to go to the kitchen, I would get a kick in the back of the legs, sending me to the floor, followed by more kicks and orders to get up.

Once the rest of the kids started to come back from

school, I would be sent to my room to wait for them to eat. Kelly thought that from now on I only needed one meal a day, and Dean would bring this to my room as he was locked in with me for the night.

One night towards the end of that week, Kelly came in and hit the covers on my bed twice with the cane. Dean had climbed into my bed after wetting his own that night. He got another two the same way, and then Kelly dragged me from under the bed and put me over the chair. She called for Dad but he wouldn't get out of bed, so, she gave me six herself.

The week drew on, with Dean staying until Saturday before moving back to his own room. I got kicked out of the house again, this time with Sarah, and told to go to my brother's for the day. It would mean a long walk, but it was a pleasant day, and; with no other way to get there, we walked the eight or so miles, stopping at the parks we passed where Sarah would rest.

Sarah slept for most of the time we were at Russell's, so I talked to him about home life. He said he would help by trying to get Mum to take Sarah for a few weeks. Then maybe we could arrange for a social worker to see her without putting her in any more danger than she already was.

Later that afternoon I spoke to Mum myself, she said that she knew I was being belted, –Dad had told her, but she didn't believe it was as often as I was trying to say. Then she went on about how I was probably bringing most of it on myself, and that I should behave better at school if I didn't want to be punished every night. I had a few tearful hours after I hung up, not understanding why she didn't believe me.

We left in plenty of time, and by my watch, arrived home five minutes early. With nothing else to do when I got in, I went to my room. I was called back to the kitchen a few minutes later and asked to explain why I was so late.

"That's seven!" Kelly shouted, pointing at the cooker clock, the minute hand on the figure seven. I tried to say the clock didn't work, but Dad shouted for me to get back to my room. He followed me in, belt already in hand.

Chapter 7

The day before I was due back at school after my suspension, I was told to have a bath. I insisted that I didn't need one, having had a shower the day before at Russell's. Kelly still thought I stank though, and dragged me to the bathroom to find Dean just getting out of the tub.

"Piss!" Kelly ordered, pointing Dean towards the bath. He did his best to follow his mother's command and dribbled over the side.

"Suzanne. Get here!" Kelly shouted as Dean left the room.

"Piss!" Kelly demanded, again, pointing at the bath as Suzanne arrived. She sat on the edge of the bath and did as she was told. Sally was still wearing nappies, so one was added to the mix before she called for Sarah.

"Piss!" she ordered yet again, pointing at the bath, but Sarah sat on the toilet.

"In there!" Kelly dragged her to the bath and held her in position over the edge. "Now!"

"I can't, I don't need to go," Sarah whimpered, and started crying. Kelly clouted her before throwing her out of the bathroom.

"Hmm, I think I need a dump," Kelly said, and readied herself on the edge of the bath and took one.

"In!" she screamed, and made a grab for me. I squirmed and managed to avoid her grip.

"Use it yourself, you might smell better, Bitch!" I shouted back at her. Dad heard and came up to see what was going on.

"Look Jacob, first the fighting and now the arsehole won't take a bath in this lovely water I've prepared for him," Kelly was saying, showing him the bath with a wave of her hand.

Dad looked in the bathtub before saying, "Go on son,

she'll leave you alone for a bit then." and headed back downstairs.

I managed to fight Kelly off until she sent me to my room. A few minutes later, I was called back and shown the bath again. The water had been changed and looked a lot cleaner, but the nappy and floating turd were still there. Also the steam coming from the surface told me the water would be scalding hot, so I still wouldn't get in when Kelly ordered. This got Dad's attention again, bringing him back to the door.

"What the fuck this time?" he bellowed.

"She's only used the hot tap Dad!" I begged.

"Too fucking right, think I'm going to pay to heat water just to cool it down for you!" Dad shouted angrily. Then he picked me up and dumped me in the bath.

He left the room straightaway but Kelly stayed for a moment, smiling at me. Once she'd closed the door, and the padlock was snapped shut, I jumped out the bath. The water had been so hot it left me red-raw from the waist down. Then the pain from the previous night's belting came back in one hit. Thankfully it soon subsided as my body cooled.

I daren't use the taps for fear of the pipes telling them I was out of the bath, so I wet the corner of a towel and washed the best I could, using water from the toilet. I knew I would be expected to clean the bath, so I waited another few minutes before emptying it.

I had just washed my hands again when Kelly came back to let me out. Picking up the nappy, I asked her what she wanted me to do with it. She put her hand underneath mine and pushed it into my face saying it was my Sunday dinner, before telling me to take it to the kitchen.

I did as I was told, washing my face again downstairs, then she came from behind and grabbed me. Taking the washing up liquid off the side, she squirted some into my mouth, followed by a load of water.

"Don't want that dirty mouth of yours saying something now, do we?" she snarled.

After I was made to gargle the mix, Kelly forced me to drink water until I threw up. Then I had to clean up the mess I'd made before being sent to my room. Dad was already there, ready to give me six belt lashes for my earlier refusal to get in the bath, and I was finally locked in for the night.

I spent most of that night catching up on my schoolwork before falling asleep under the bed. Kelly woke me in the morning with a bucket of water. I got dressed and made breakfast for the kids, and after all the bowls were cleared I walked Sarah to school.

Mine and Sarah's schools were on the same grounds, and, as we came close to the gate, Tony jumped from behind the wall. It looked to me as if he was going for Sarah rather than myself though, so I shouted. "Oi! Aren't you hard enough to take me on again then? Well, are you?" then I made a run for it.

Tony chased me around the corner for a minor scuffle, making us a few minutes late, so we both got sent to the head's office. I was called in first and only avoided another suspension because I had managed to get my schoolwork up to date. He still gave me two from the cane for fighting, then told me to wait for Tony before I went back to my classes. Within a few minutes Tony came back out, after taking his own cane strikes, and told me that he was now my guide for the school. So now we would have to get along or both get suspended.

Then he showed me around, pointing out where the smokers would be, and the toilets where I had to deliver my non-existent lunch money daily. We had several scuffles in there until he realised I really didn't get any. He also shared most of my classes, leaving me only Maths and Physics without being called names throughout the whole lesson.

Kelly seemed surprised I was so late back home that day. She had been expecting me to get expelled for not having my schoolwork done on time. I told her that I said it had been stolen on the way to school, but the head was going to let me catch up in detentions, another thing I came home with.

After the other kids had eaten, and with the washing up was done, Kelly dragged me to my room to wait for Dad. When he came in a little later, he already knew about the fight with Tony. I tried to explain that he was going to attack Sarah, but Dad wouldn't listen and ordered the chair to the middle of the room. Asking how many I got at school, he told me I should have got double, so I was caned another four times that night before the door was locked again.

The following day started much the same way, though I managed to avoid Tony until we got onto the school grounds. We had sports that day, and Tony had threatened to break my leg during the football we'd be playing. I wasn't too scared about that, but my legs still hurt from the caning, so I claimed I had forgotten my kit.

The gym teacher said to get undressed anyway, as it was an indoor five-a-side lesson, so I could do it in my underwear, then disappeared into his office. Coming back a few minutes later, he changed his mind, because, boys that get caned can be excused from sports for a few days, and that I should have just told him.

I still got a detention for forgetting my kit, and so was late back to the house again. All the other kids had eaten and gone out for the evening. So when I got in, Kelly ordered me to the bottom step without even coming out the living room.

I stood there for maybe an hour before Dad came in and asked about my day. I told him about the sports lesson and was sent to my room. Kelly came up a few minutes later to tell me she was going to get Dad to cane me for something, but I didn't see either of them again that night.

Wednesday's breakfast went the same way, but I held back from going through the school gates because Tony was waiting there. He stayed until well after the bell that called us to the morning registration had gone off, so, already in trouble, I went to the local park. Someone called me by name and took me back to school, then on to the head's office, where he warned me that I was on thin ice with bunking off added to my list of crimes.

That night, it was clear by the look on Dad's face that he knew how my day had been. I walked past him saying I would see him in my room. He followed me in a few minutes later to give me six lashes with the cane. I pulled up my trousers, feeling the fresh burning pain down the back of my legs, and rolled under the bed for a few hours.

Kelly came in at some point after I had fallen asleep, and dragged me by the hair from under the bed, screaming that if I didn't want a bed I shouldn't have one. Then she grabbed the headboard, flipping the bed on top of me, and walked out locking the door behind her. The bed wasn't heavy but, the way it landed on my hip hurt like hell and gave me a limp that would last for a few days.

I really wasn't feeling up to anything the following morning, so I tried to make myself so late that I would be kept off school. Kelly threw me out the house in the end, and I arrived for my first lesson half an hour late.

Tony repeated his threats about breaking my leg, so I went to see the school nurse during break. She to a look at my hip and said it was nothing to worry about but excused me from sports for a few days. When I got back to class, Tony seemed to know that I'd been excused from sports, but still kept his threats going.

Later that day, when I saw him chatting to some of

the lads who had beaten me up, I ran over and barged him so hard that he fell backwards down some stairs. I soon followed him, as his mates pushed me down.

When I climbed off Tony, he was unconscious and it was clear his leg had been broken in the fall. I looked up the stairs just in time to watch his mates run off in various directions. Then I set the fire alarm off. Some teachers found me, still with Tony, as they carried out the fire drill and evacuated the school.

I was told to go to the head's office after admitting to fighting with Tony, saying we rolled down the stairs together, with him taking the brunt of the fall, before I set the alarm off. Though he commended me on my honesty and actions; I was still suspended until he had carried out an investigation, to prove I wasn't the cause of the accident by setting the alarm off first.

I wanted to wait for Dad to get home that night, so I went to the park after leaving school, planning on going back to the house about half an hour before the other kids were due in. Although I knew that I was probably in for a bad time just for being in early. I hoped this would give me my best chance to explain before Dean told them a different story of why I was suspended again.

When I did get back home, Dad was waiting behind the door and punched me in the face so hard I fell back out again.

"Fucking suspended? What for this fucking time?" Dad bellowed, as I started to get to my knees.

He pulled me into the house by my shoulders and threw me in Kelly's direction. She tossed me to the kitchen floor and kicked me between the legs. I shouted up at them that there had been an accident at school where I fell down the stairs. Dad got me to my feet and told me to explain myself. I went through what I had earlier told the head, before adding that someone wanted to see me the next day, about the investigation the school was carrying out.

I was locked in my room for a few hours, then I heard the padlock get taken off my door and Kelly shouted for me. She was stood at the top of the stairs and told me to show her what had happened at school that day.

I looked at her, and then the stairs, but she caught me by surprise, pushing me off balance. I tumbled down head over heels, rolling into the toilet door at the bottom. Then she shouted for me to get back up to the top because I hadn't fallen right.

I stumbled back up the stairs, a little bruised but not hurting too bad. She met me part way from the top and dragged me up the last few steps. Her grip then moved from my throat to the back of my neck.

I was a little more prepared this time, and half-dived when she pushed, going down the stairs on my belly most of the way, adding a few carpet burns to what was becoming a painful body.

"No, no, no," Kelly was saying, coming down the stairs to grab me again. "We must try harder this time." We were on our way back up.

At the top she grabbed my belt and threw me back down the stairs. This time, I hit semi-upright about halfway down, badly twisting my ankle, before ending in a crumpled heap at the bottom.

"That'll do," Kelly said, walking past me and back to the living room.

I crawled back upstairs to my room and under the bed. Hearing the lock snap shut a few minutes later, I closed my eyes and tried to will away the pain.

The man that turned up the following day spoke to Kelly at length before coming to give me the good news. He thought that Kelly's explanation of my nightmare, and sleepwalking accident the night before, was in my favour, so he would see what he could do to have my suspension lifted. Then he said thank you and his goodbyes' without asking me a single question.

Kelly locked my door shortly after he left, and, I

spent the next three or four days in bed. Sarah would bring me some food every now and then, and keep me company for a half-hour or so while I ate.

About a week later, Dean warned me that his mum was up to something, so I took to sleeping under the bed again. A few nights after that, Kelly stood at the door with her hands on her hips saying, "Well, shall we see if we're strong enough yet? Chair!"

"What for?" I shouted back, having not left my room in days.

"Well, there's two for not doing what you're told, and...," Kelly paused to think, "...yes, I think another two for answering me back. Now move it!" If I spoke after that, Kelly added two more to my total, calling for Dad when she got to twelve.

"This little shit has disobeyed me for the last fucking time Jacob. Now he owes me twelve, so fucking well get on with it," she shouted when Dad came in.

"Come on son, let's get this over with," Dad said, checking the number while taking off his belt.

I picked up the chair and threw it at the window; my ankle may have hurt like hell but I had every intention of jumping out when the glass smashed. I had hold of the frame with both hands and was shouting for help before they got hold of me.

Dad had managed to get my legs, while Kelly prised my fingers free, then as soon as I hit the floor she sat on my back, pinning me where I fell. Dad let go of me, and inspected the damage; seconds later he was off to see what boards he had for the broken window. I was still screaming for help as loud as I could, but Kelly pulled one of my socks off. Forcing it into my mouth, she then stayed sat on my back until Dad finished boarding up the window.

"Right! Now you're going to fucking get it!" Dad sneered down at me as he went for the cane.

By the time Dad came back, Kelly had already thrown me over the chair. Then she told him to sit on me while she went to find something. He straddled me, not with all his weight, but enough to make breathing through a sock almost impossible. Then Kelly made it worse, coming back with a tie she used as a gag.

"We don't want the neighbours hearing now, do we?" she whispered in my ear as she took my arms and pulled my shoulders into the chair legs.

With the first lash, I heard the whistling noise, and knew it was going to hurt a lot more than usual. It landed just below my buttocks and felt like it had cut through to the bone; the next two were no better – first over my thighs followed by the bottom of my back. Everything went dark.

I'm not sure how long it was before I came round, still gagged and lying over the chair. The back of my legs felt like someone had used a cheese grater on them for a few hours. I peered at the vicious red lines, which seemed to glow in the dim light, by my count I had taken at least eight. After pulling up my trousers I crawled under the bed and hoped that was it for the night.

A little later, I thought I was having a bad dream, seeing Kelly on her hands and knees looking under the bed for me. Then she threw some water over my face, bringing me back to reality.

"You should use that glass over there, it will hurt you less!" she sneered, pointing in the direction of the window.

It was a Saturday morning, after being locked in my room for over four weeks; Dad opened the door and tossed fifty pence at me, then told me to get out and find Sarah. She was in the garden, so it didn't take much looking, and soon I was hobbling away from the house with her.

She insisted that she wanted to go to Russell's that

day. I spent the next hour trying to explain that we didn't have enough money for the bus fare and that I couldn't walk that far with my ankle. She convinced me to try, bursting into tears, so in the end I gave in and took her.

It was me that wanted to stop on every seat we passed this time, and it took some hours to get there. Nonetheless, we made it and my worst fears were put to rest when we found he was in. Russell asked about the limp I had so, I showed him my ankle – now lots of shades of yellow, blue and black. Later he showed me how to strap it with a bandage, then watched me a few times until he was confident that I could do it myself.

Later that day, I was in my underwear after taking a shower when Russell asked how I'd burned myself. I was confused at first, and then corrected him, saying that I had been caned a few nights before. He tried to count how many marks there were, but couldn't tell the old from the new, and so never arrived at a number. But he gave me some cream for the tender skin, which was a big help.

Leaving Russell's with plenty of time to spare, I got home to an empty house. In my room the boards over the window had been replaced with glass, the painted putty still soft. I etched 'help us now' into it with a blunt pencil, and crawled under my bed, exhausted.

It was about five weeks after my accident with the stairs before I went back to school. My ankle was still pretty sore but the strapping was a big help. Tony would be off for a few more weeks with his leg, and none of his mates would come near me for a while, which was a bonus.

That let me settle into a few classes, and during one Maths lesson I showed off a trick I'd learnt in my last school, beating other pupils on a multiplication question without using a calculator. It impressed the girl I sat next to so much that she asked to meet me later. I was nervous when I went to the place she had said, thinking it was another set-up; but when I got there she was alone.

Clare was a very sweet girl and always had a smile on her face. She was about the same build as me, and though she was six months younger, she had ended up in my year's intake. In the end she would stand up to anyone that bullied me and we had lots of good times together. But at first I would only see her at school, where we kept each other company during breaks.

Over the next few months, things were much the same. Two or three times a week I would be accused of something and get belted or caned, normally a grounding to think about what I'd done would follow. The few times I did get out I'd go to Clare's.

Kelly then started to get Dean to follow me, so I would run off as fast as my battered body would let me. He was faster than me at the sprint, but I could run further, so I had a fair chance of getting away.

Somehow, he still found out where Clare lived and would wait outside her house for me to leave. One time, when I saw him out the window, I jumped over Clare's back fence and ran home.

"Where the fuck's Dean?" Kelly screamed as I came in.

"I don't know! Last time I saw him he was smoking up at the shops!" I shouted back at her.

She smacked me round the face so hard I was thrown into the cooker. Then, pushing me through the door, she kicked me in the direction of the stairs. But that was nothing to what happened when Dean came in.

It sounded like he hit the cooker the same way as I did, as Kelly started shouting about how she could smell cigarette smoke on him, probably with a fag in her own hand. Then he got thrown into the cupboards for being stupid enough to get caught, before being locked in with me for the night. He was only semi-conscious when he arrived, and couldn't remember much of what actually happened to him.

School was okay for a few months. Tony had learned that he could get hurt just as bad as I could, and this kept him at bay for a while. I still struggled with lessons, mainly because at my old school they had used a different set of exercise books, but I managed to stay about average in most subjects.

I got into a lot of minor trouble, with regular visits to the head's office for a chat. Thankfully, he wasn't a great believer in the cane, so he only used it if I'd been in a fight, otherwise he would give out a week of detentions. I had a lot of these, but also a lot fewer fights after school, so less caning overall.

During the weekends or holidays, I was often thrown a coin by Dad and told to get out of the house with Sarah. I had to talk her out of going to Russell's every time. It was too far for her to walk really, so I would take her round the town for hours on end instead.

We weren't allowed back to the house until the evening though, finding the doors locked if we got back early, and with only enough money for a drink between us, I took to shoplifting for food. I'm so glad Sarah wasn't with me when I got caught.

I was so hungry after not being fed for two days that I stole a Yorkie bar from Woolworths. I begged for the manager to forgive me and not to call anyone. But he thought I was lying about who I was, because I didn't know the house number I lived at, so he called the police.

When they picked me up they drove to my house but no one seemed to be in when the officer knocked. He left a note then carried on to the station, questioning me when we arrived. I had stopped trying any excuses, and admitted that I stole the chocolate because I was hungry. Then Dad arrived and was called into the interview room.

We went through my statement again for Dad, but were pretty much done before he had arrived. The officer then said he was happy that I had learnt my lesson, and seeing as this was my first reported offence, he was happy to release me into Dad's discipline.

He had barely finished speaking before Dad had me bent over the desk. He got in at least twelve hard smacks before one of the officers grabbed his arm and said that was enough. Dad grabbed my arm and pulled me out of the room, then I was dragged through the station, with him swearing at me the whole time.

When we got home I didn't need to be told, and I ran up the stairs to get ready on the chair. I knew it would be the cane, and learning from the previous gagging, I stuffed a clean sock in my mouth, which also helped to control the pain. Eight across the back of my legs later, I spat out the sock, thinking it was all over.

Dad had other ideas, telling me to stand up and hold my hands out one at a time, and I got another six across each of my palms. My hands swelled so badly, I couldn't hold a pen for a few days. I made sure I didn't get caught stealing again after that.

The money I saved by shoplifting allowed me to send Sarah swimming every few weeks; I wouldn't bother myself. I always had strap or cane marks across my back and legs, and didn't want people talking under their breath about me. A few times Clare came with us to keep me company while I waited though, which was nice.

One time outside the swimming baths, Dean saw us together just as Sarah came out. He shouted that he was going to tell Dad that I had a girlfriend, and threw a stone in our direction.

I didn't even hear it land before I was after him, tripping him over, a hundred yards or so down the road. Someone shouted, so I went back to see how the girls were. Clare started shouting at me before I was even close, saying that Sarah was hurt. I quickened my pace to see what had happened.

Sarah had a little cut and a big bump on her head, so we took her to a friend's house on the way back. Adam's mum had a look at her, and thought it was nothing too serious, just needing a plaster.

We still stayed there for a while until Sarah had stopped complaining about her headache, then Sarah and I walked home with Adam's mum. She explained our side of the story before leaving us in the living room. After she left, Dad called for Dean.

"Throw stones at my daughter, will you!" Dad shouted at Dean when he came to the door; then taking his belt off he turned to me and shouted, "Down!"

I kept my jeans on, but, still took six of his best over the arm of the sofa, before being sent to the back garden. Dean joined me on the grass a few minutes later after taking a few lashes himself. Dad and Kelly followed, arguing about which of their sons' would win in a fair fight. But the way Kelly was taking up position behind me; I knew that this fight was going to be a long way from fair.

As soon as the shout went up, I spun on my heels and caught Kelly in the kidney as she grabbed me in a bear hug. Dean jumped on my back at the same time, sending the three of us to the ground. Kelly was up first, leaving Dean and me to roll around for a minute or so; then she got hold of one of my arms.

I tried to stop her getting my other arm, but only managed for a few seconds. Kelly pulled me to my feet and forced both arms up my back. Then ordering Dean to punch me in the belly, it wasn't long before I could barely breathe.

Kelly soon let go, claiming Dean to be the winner. As she did, I dived for Dean in a rugby tackle, taking him to the ground again. A couple of punches to his ribs and face later, I was dragged off him by Kelly and thrown across the garden. Then Dad grabbed me, and took me up to my room, locking me in.

The ambulance arrived about ten minutes later, and, Dean spent the next few days in hospital with a punctured lung. When Kelly came back from the hospital a few hours later, she said that she was going to move out, and taking her girls she left again.

Chapter 8

The few days without Kelly were the best I spent in the house. The cupboards were unlocked and, although I still had to fend for Sarah and myself, there were no restrictions on how much food we ate.

We were on half-term from school too, and I remember getting enough money from Dad to take Sarah off to the pictures one afternoon. Seeing her holding a Coke cup that was as big as she was, stuffing her face with popcorn and trying to smile all at the same time, was hilarious, and made it all worth it, just for those few hours.

All this ended the day Kelly came back and announced that she was pregnant, then demanded that I owed her thirty lashes for hitting a woman in her condition. I'm glad even Dad thought this was a bit much: fifteen from the belt ended the row they were having about it.

The next day, Dean told Tony that I had been softened up for him, and a few days later I met Tony and four of his mates at the school gates. They instantly had the better of me, letting me know to be more careful near the stairs in the future.

Clare saw them start on me and ran over. Still at full speed, she barged two of them off me and I managed to get away. But it was seen by the head, and won me my first suspension during Kelly's pregnancy. Now I would spend all my time scrubbing the house because she had decided to have the baby at home.

On the second or third day of my suspension, while I was scrubbing the kitchen floor with neat bleach, Kelly pushed me into one of the cupboard doors, saying, "Wait till your Dad hears about this!" while she wafted a letter in my face. Dad got back about an hour after the other kids got in from school. Then we all got called to the living room.

"Right you fuckers!" Kelly was sneering as we lined up against the wall.

"We've got the fucking social here tomorrow because of this little shit!" Pointing at me, she carried on, "If any of you little fucks says one fucking word out of line you'll all get what he's getting now!" Then she grabbed me by the hair and threw me towards the chair from my room, which was now in front of the fire.

I'd given up trying to fight them off, so I dropped my trousers and hoped for the best. Then Dad seemed to manage to hit the same spot on my legs with all six lashes from the cane, before Kelly dragged me to my feet. Telling me it wasn't over yet, she threw me towards the fireplace. As much as I could, I aimed to hit my head on the shelf to knock myself out and stop the pain.

I was a bit groggy after my knock, but I know it was Kelly who put the bag over my face. I don't know if I passed out or not, but when I couldn't get a breath I lashed out, and Sarah fell back with a bloody nose. She was crying, with Kelly shouting at her to come back with the bag when I took a kick in the side, I think from Dad.

Then Sarah was ordered to hold the bag over my face until I stopped fighting. Poor Sarah was in tears while the other kids and Kelly shouted, "Do it! Do it!"

I tried to smile and say it was okay for her to do as she was told. I only remember one more kick in the leg after that, before being dragged out of bed the following morning.

The next day I remember doing breakfast for the kids, but not much else. There's also a vague memory of a figure, a man I assumed, by the sound of the voice, standing in my doorway and talking about pneumonia and babies.

Then I know I was dragged around the house at some point, but only because I remember Sarah helped me back to my room when she came home from school. She was saying something about Russell, and sure enough, the following morning it came back to me.

Pouring with rain I was given twenty pence and kicked out of the house with Sarah. I did have my senses back, but my body was a wreck. The weeping lash marks on my legs made every step agonising, and my chest was so tight I couldn't take a full breath. Walking slowly next to me, Sarah stopped asking to go to Russell's.

We made our way to Clare's instead, and with her parents asleep the house was very quiet. It gave me time to put some cream on my legs and for me to speak to Sarah about what had happened.

She thought I had been there for another hour, but it was probably a lot less. I had passed out in front of the fire with Kelly sat on my chest shouting what the other kids were to say the following day. Every few words, she slapped me round the face until her speech finished. Then Dean helped Sarah to get me upstairs.

We stayed with Clare for a few hours, and got home about the same time we would've done if we'd gone to Russell's. In the kitchen, I saw that I was owed six by Kelly's clock so, I found myself looking at Dad's feet. I could tell by his gesture that he meant me to go to my room. He followed me in a few moments later.

"You've had enough for now son," he said quietly. "Squeal like a pig, you'll know when." Then he bellowed something so loud that the room shook, but I could still hear the cane whip through the air.

The shock of it hitting the bed instead of me made me cheer so loud that I think Dad got the desired effect. He hit the bed five more times, each followed by a more believable scream. Six bed lashes later, I was still crying through relief rather than pain; then Dad winked and left me alone to rest.

After an uneventful Sunday, I was still struggling to breathe on Monday morning back at school, so Clare talked me into seeing the nurse. She was a kind, pretty woman, and we talked about my concerns. She seemed to think I had a slightly collapsed chest, and considered it a common injury from the rugby we were now learning during sports. Asking about the lash marks, I explained that I was caned a lot. I don't think she realised that I hadn't been at school for the last two weeks.

By now it obviously had got back to Dad that I had a girlfriend. He thought that I was too young to have friendships like that, and banned me from seeing Clare at all. This was impossible to do at school, of course, so Dean would come back with stories about what he had seen me doing with her, which got me belted daily.

Then one day, I was sent to see the nurse as my year had our vaccinations updated. All the girls had their MMR jabs, with the boys also being treated to the cough and drop test. When I got home that night, Dad was fuming at me for showing myself to Clare behind the bike sheds; the story Dean had told him.

I was shouting all the way upstairs that it had been a medical and that Clare wasn't even at school that day, but he wanted to teach me a lesson anyway. Biting down on the sock in my mouth, the first six lashes came so fast I almost lost count. I thought that was it, and started to relax; Sarah counted twelve later that night, although I only remembered two more.

I spent the next three days with my jeans sticking to the weeping marks across the back of my legs. I could hardly walk for the pain, so I was kept off school. When I did go back I got suspended again because they thought I'd bunked off.

A few weeks after I went back to school, with Kelly ruling the house with an iron rod, there was a nit infestation. So the nurse came round checking pupil's hair, helped by a few of the teachers; the nurse herself checked me.

I didn't have any nits, but Tony had a few. He spent the rest of the day telling me that nits were only found in clean hair, so, I was still a smelly shit; I had to laugh at that one for a while. Dean had nits too and once we got home from school we were treated to a vicious razor-comb haircut from Dad, followed by a hair wash from Kelly with ethanol shampoo.

I was the last to get my hair washed and there was no shampoo left. Instead, Kelly picked up the bottle of bleach next to the toilet and rubbed a good load of it into my scalp. I kept my eyes squeezed closed but it didn't stop them stinging like hell. A minute or so later she rinsed it off with ice cold water, but by twisting my head from side to side I managed to get any bleach away from my eyes.

What hair I had left in the morning was bright yellow, and when Kelly saw it, she held me on my chair so Dad could shave my head with a razor. Dad left me with a few nicks that were still bleeding when I got to school. Later that day, when they called Dad, he told them I had panicked about the nits and must have done it to myself. The head decided to suspend me, for the third time in four months, until my hair had grown back.

Back at home, Kelly would try to order me from here to there, but I exaggerated the pain I was in from my regular beating sessions. Instead I got plenty of kicks off her and a lot of time in my room. A few days later, Dad packed me off to a mate of his to get rid of me.

Joshua was going to look after me for the last week of my suspension, promising that I would come back a different boy. He lived on a fixed caravan site, but wasn't what you would call a traveller. He had worked with Dad years before and they had never lost touch. Standing about six feet tall, and even at the age of twelve, I would have said he sounded feminine. I didn't want to go, but I hoped it might be a chance for me to talk to someone who would listen.

I had been there about three days, when Joshua took me to the centre of the estate where he lived for some lunch. On the way back he suggested we stop at a pub as a treat for me behaving so well for him.

We took a seat, towards the back of the bar, and talking gently Joshua said that he could tell I wasn't having a great time at home, so if I wanted to talk, he would listen. I burst into tears, so he hugged me for a moment and then went for some drinks.

Coming back with half a lager for me, he tried to stop my tears. Then I think we talked about how I got more punishment than Dean for the same crimes, but he did get me a few more drinks, so it all gets a bit cloudy.

I know I was crying all the time we spoke, so when he offered to go back to the caravan, it sounded like a better idea than everyone in the pub seeing me ball my eyes out.

I went to the toilet to give my face a quick wash before we left. As I was relieving myself, Joshua joined me at the urinal trough.

"There-there, boy," he said, and made a move for my groin. "Let me hold that for you."

I caught his thumb just as his hand came close to me, and pushed it so hard towards his wrist that I heard it pop. Then I ran out of the pub, leaving Joshua in the toilets, screaming.

I didn't have a clue where I was, apart from town somewhere, so I was running in circles trying to find a landmark. It felt like hours before the police picked me up and took me back to the house, still half-drunk.

As soon as the police car pulled away, Kelly dragged me to my room and ordered me to be sick in a bucket. I refused to stick my fingers down my own throat, so she forced nearly my whole hand in my mouth until I puked up. Then, with the bucket a quarter full, she ordered me to drink it; but as soon as she picked it up I knocked the bottom, spilling it everywhere.

Then I started screaming about what happened in the pub as Dad came in shouting, "Shut the fuck up!" I had dislocated Joshua's thumb.

Twelve very painful lashes later, I was thanking myself for still having my wits about me, given what might have happened if I had fallen asleep there that night.

Chapter 9

After my close call with Joshua, I had to get some kind of plan together. The amount of punishment I was going through at home, and the school bullying, plus a possible paedophile to contend with, was too much. I needed help fast.

I had tried to get help from Russell before, but he had moved by then and we'd lost touch. I hadn't seen Mum for over a year, having never been allowed to visit her because of one thing or another. She was likely to talk to Dad anyway, and I didn't want to take the chance of another bad beating off him. So I went to the only other place I could think of – Nan's.

Nan was a sweet old lady, though she could get very abusive if she took a dislike to someone. At the time she would have been sixty-something and suffered with dementia, so she could get a bit random at times. This was something I knew well, but she also put many a smile on my face over the years.

I had dropped Sarah off with Clare for a day out swimming, before going to Nan's alone. When I arrived she seemed a little more upset than normal, probably because she thought her meals-on-wheels lady was late. As it turned out she wasn't due that day, but with plenty in her cupboards I got on and made her some lunch.

My uncle Peter, who was the real reason for my visit, called on her daily, so I tidied around the small flat, knowing Nan couldn't do it herself. As we chatted, she would often call me Peter, so I reminded her who I was a few times, grinning to myself.

"Yes, I know you're Dave, you silly boy, Peter. You're Dona's boy aren't you?" she said, referring to my Mum by name.

Then, waving her finger at me like I was being told off, she carried on, "And that man should have nothing to do with you Dave, you hear? That Jacob, he's not your Dad, you know. Now you get away from him Peter boy. He's no good, and I told your mum, so you know I did. Hurt him I said, and now look, he did too, didn't he?"

I was gobsmacked, but also confused about who she was talking about – Peter or me? He arrived a few minutes later, and with little time to go through everything, I asked him what Nan was going on about.

Peter then was like me now – tall and skinny, and we share many similar facial features – but with well over twenty years between us he thought Nan should be able to tell us apart.

Once I told him what she had said, he dug into his pocket and gave me a ten-pound note, telling me to speak to Mum first, because if I didn't know yet, it wasn't his place to tell me. I had to go then; the money may have saved a nine-mile run but, I was still cutting it close with buses to meet Sarah on time.

Sarah and Clare were just about to leave the swimming pool when I got back to meet them. I held Clare back a few steps on the walk home and talked about my day. She seemed to understand how confused I was, and agreed to come with me to meet my mum.

It took two weeks of daily belting's and fights at school before I arrived at Mum's front door, holding Clare's hand. I explained that Sarah was ill when she asked, so she wouldn't go on about why I hadn't brought her. In fact I didn't want Sarah to know what I was about to ask, so I'd dropped her off at a friend's house.

We were invited in, and I introduced Clare to Mum's new husband, Karl, and my aunt Daisy. I didn't know that my aunt would be visiting that weekend, but I had come too far to turn back now, so I soon started to talk about my visit with Nan a few weeks earlier.

"Oh, did she?" Mum said, after I had finished

recounting the conversation I had with Nan.

"Is that all you've got to say?" I asked.

"She's losing her mind Dave, so she was probably confusing you with someone else," Mum replied.

"Who is my father then..., Jacob, Karl?" I yelled.

"Your father isn't the man who made you Dave. He is the man that loves and creates you. Do you understand that?" Daisy offered, trying to calm things down.

"What!" Clare shouted at the top of her voice, and after lifting my shirt, she went on. "Does this look like a father's love to you? Now shut up and answer him!"

Clare hugged me, urging me to ask again.

"Is Jacob my father?" I whispered, sobbing, already knowing the answer.

"Is he my dad..., Mum?" I asked again, raising my voice. A moment later Mum burst into tears and buried her head in her hands.

"Who the fuck is my father, you *BITCH*?" I shouted at the top of my voice. "Well, are you going to tell me or not?"

Mum never raised her head as she said, "No."

As I heard the word, my legs gave way. Then I pushed myself across the floor into the corner of the room, and cried into my knees. Clare came and sat next to me, keeping everyone else away if they tried to come too close. Not that I was about to listen to any of them now. I was so angry at how I could have been left there so long, with a man that wasn't even my father, and I was already thinking that I was beaten, only because I wasn't his kid.

I don't know how long I sat there before Clare led me to the bathroom. She helped me wash and re-strap my chest for the suspected bust rib I had. Then, after I had re-strapped my ankle, I asked Clare to unlock the door so Daisy could see in.

"Oh my god Dave, how long?" Daisy asked as I turned full circle, wearing only my underwear, showing her my red raw legs from the belt or cane, and bruises head to toe.

"Six years!" I looked at her, then closed the door to dress.

Mum and Daisy were talking about what should be done with me when I came back into the living room. They'd already called the social and said I was to see them the next weekend at Mum's.

"You've got two hours to get Sarah, then, haven't you?" I stated rather angrily.

"What?" Daisy asked, a little shocked.

I explained to her that I had to keep Sarah with me to stop me running off and doing exactly what I was doing now. She may have been a brave girl, but keeping secrets from Kelly wasn't anyone's strongest point.

"You'll have to hurry if you need to get her home Dave..., I'll see if I've got the bus fare for you," Mum said, reaching into her bag.

"What the fuck! You want me to go back! Now? ...After hearing all this!" I shouted at her.

"Think what he'll do to Sarah if you don't!" Daisy's voice contained both menace and fear.

I took a few moments to look at each of them in turn, wondering how they could let Sarah stay there after seeing how battered I was. But if they weren't going to take her in, I had to go back, or she would be asked where I was with no answers to give them, and they knew it.

"I'll go," I said, and got up to leave.

They stopped me before I got to the door and gave me a fair amount of money; I passed it all to Clare to look after. Then Daisy walked us to the bus stop suggesting excuses I could use about where I'd been all day. I wasn't listening.

On the ride home, I sat at the back of the bus sharing pie and chips with Clare. I didn't realise until she handed me a tissue that I was still streaming tears. As I took it off her and wiped my eyes dry, it hit me – what am I going to tell Sarah? I buried my head into Clare's shoulder and cried uncontrollably.

"When this is over," I said once I got some control back, "I'm going to change my name to Dave Frost and marry you. You're the only family I have now." She hugged me, hiding another wave of tears.

I didn't come to my senses again until we arrived in town. I was nearly an hour late already and the bus I needed next had just left. Waiting for the next one was out the question because Sarah, would be panicking or worse still, would already have gone home.

I really didn't care what happened to me now, so I sprinted the two and a half miles, all uphill, with Clare panting in the distance behind me. When I got to the house Sarah should have been at, I was gasping for air. A few deep breaths later, Clare caught up and I asked for Sarah.

"Oh, she went to the park with Adam. Then her other brother came and took her home," his mum told us.

I shared a look of horror with Clare. Over an hour and a half late and Sarah taken home by Dean, we both knew I wouldn't be able to walk for a week.

I went for the door, but Clare blocked the way. I begged her to let me go, but she stood holding the frame. Then as I went to give her a hug I saw her let go, so I pushed past and was out of the door, running for home before she could catch me again. I stopped about a hundred yards away from my house; seconds later Clare joined me.

"Look!" I said, pointing towards the house. "There's a light on in my room. They're waiting for me!"

"Dave, don't do it," Clare was saying, with tears in her eyes.

"Okay, but you know I've got to get Sarah. She was in the front bedroom the last I knew, so I'll get her to jump out the window." Seeing Clare nod, I edged towards the house.

I tried to stay out of sight until I got to the top of the garden path. Then, looking about on the ground, I found a few small stones and started throwing them at Sarah's window. Three or four attempts later, the curtains parted and Kelly opened the window.

"Well young man, if you want to see your sister again you'd better get in here," she sneered down at me before shouting to Dad that I was back. I looked up the road and blew Clare a kiss, then walked down the path and into the house.

As soon as I got in the back door, Dad's hand covered my face and he lifted me off the ground. My feet didn't touch the floor again until he threw me over the chair in my room and went for the cane. I knew I was in for a bad time for being caught without Sarah, but I didn't expect what happened next.

"So...," Dad said, walking around the room. "Did we enjoy ourselves with that whore?" I bit down on the sock in my mouth and said a silent prayer. "Think we're old enough to lose our virginity now? Do we?" Dad seemed so calm.

Whoosh, the cane hit the bottom of my back.

I was holding onto the chair for dear life but couldn't help myself arching backwards. The next one hit me across the shoulder blades, sending me back over the chair. My whole body was in pain, and I don't know where the cane strikes hit next. I knew they were hitting, but they seemed to hit everywhere all at once.

"So...," Two lashes, "think you can have...," two more, "sex with that bitch!" Dad relayed Dean's story.

Two more lashes, I went limp and passed out. I was still draped over the chair I don't know how long later. Sarah was in front of me saying sorry and trying to get me to drink something. She felt it was her fault that I was in trouble. I smiled as best as I could and said it wasn't her. Then she leant towards me and took a flannel from the back of my neck.

"What happened?" I whimpered as she doused the cloth in some bloodied water.

"Dad got so angry at you. He broke his cane and couldn't find the other one so he carried on with his belt," she whispered back.

"Just the thin ones, how many?" I asked, telling her where to find my cream. Sarah started to count from the neck down; by the time she got to my hips she had got to thirty. I couldn't listen to her crying any more so I had to ask her to stop.

I stayed as still as I could over the chair for days after that, being fed by Sarah and drinking with a straw. If I tried to move my arms or legs they would burn as if they were on fire.

My saving grace for now was that Dad had realised he had gone way too far this time. The broken cane and the belt were thrown out that night. Sarah dug the belt out of the bin and gave it to me to hide so he wouldn't use it again. Dad didn't use his new belt on me for a while, but I did feel his hand again soon after. And with the state I was in, even that was too much.

Then I phoned Mum on what I thought was the following Saturday to say I couldn't make it across.

She told me the social had been the week before, so I wasn't to worry, because now they were looking into my case, so it wouldn't be long before I was away from the house. I got the same line for the following couple of weeks, and finally gave up on the social ever coming for me.

About five weeks later I got caught red-handed kissing Clare after school. Kelly had walked past just as we were saying goodbye for the night. The look she gave me across the road told me what would happen when I got home. I was terrified, but there was no way I was going to leave Sarah in that house.

Clare tried to hold me back but I got away from her and ran off, only stopping at the end of my garden path. Dad was stood by the front door, with Kelly telling him what she'd seen; I really didn't fancy getting killed this time, so I didn't go down the path. Then, when Clare caught up, we started shouting at each other across the garden.

"If you're going to beat me!" I shouted at Dad and Kelly, noticing some neighbours listening to what was going on. "Come on, get the chair and we'll do it here!"

"Fuck him off Jacob! He's not yours anyway so let that bitch have him." Kelly shouted at Dad, then turned back to me. "You hear that! Did you? He's not your father. You're just a fucking one night stand that got dumped on us, so go on, fuck off, and don't come back!"

Dad looked up and started to chase us off. He gave up after only a few steps, adding his own "fuck off" to the total, as me and Clare disappeared up the road.

We arrived at her house hand in hand, with me in floods of tears, so her mum called me to her asking what had upset me so much. She listened as I spoke about my last few weeks waiting for the social to call, and what was likely to happen if I went home. It wasn't long before she had arranged for me to go to the social office the following morning.

It took nearly two weeks before I told the social everything I'd been through over the past few years. Then one day when I called in to their office, a worker said "Ah Dave, take a seat."

Leading me into her office she continued. "Your stepfather has been down and said he's sorry for the way you found out about him not being your real father. He's willing to try to make it up to you if you would only consent to going back home."

"Yeah right, got a new cane he wants to try out then

has he?" I answered back.

"Dave, there's no need to be like that."

"Look!" I said abruptly. "I've told you what happens when they even think I've spoken to you lot. I ain't going back to find out what will happen when I have."

"Okay." She began to give in. "We've contacted your Mum and she can take you in, but only when she moves to a bigger house. It might take a few weeks, so you can stay where you are for now."

"I don't want to go to Mum's, so just look for foster parents nearby." I was adamant that I didn't want to be far away from Sarah.

I stayed at Clare's for another month or so, going to the social every few days and adding to my statement. Mum found a bigger house, so was busy arranging the move, but we talked on the phone most days. I eventually changed my mind, deciding to go to her, with promises of regular visits to Sarah and Clare. Then all too soon the day arrived to leave Clare's arrived.

"Where's Sarah?" I asked the social worker who picked me up, knowing that she wanted to see me off.

"We thought it would be better not to bring her today," he answered, opening the car door for me. "And besides, you'll be seeing her at the weekend."

"But Sarah was going to help me move in. It was all arranged, so can we go and pick her up please?" I said as I got into the car.

"I've been instructed to take you to your Mum's and nowhere else. Sorry." He said, checking my seatbelt was okay.

"But—," I started, but the closing door cut me short.

"Look, she's not your sister anymore and, I'm not even sure where she'll be right now, so the answer is no," he said, getting into the driver's seat and closing his own door.

I tried to open my door but the child lock was on, so I wound down the window and went for the handle outside. By the time my fingers touched it we were speeding down the road. I did think about opening the door anyway, but soon changed my mind, and spent the whole trip to Mum's crying on the back seat.

When I got there I went straight to Mum, demanding to go back for Sarah. She sat me down and explained that it had been her idea not to bring her. Because it was the day she and Karl were moving into the new house, she wouldn't be able to keep an eye on the both of us, and with boxes all over the place I could see her point of view and quietened down quickly.

Karl was Scottish, and had married Mum a year or so after she had left Dad. I had met him a few times on visits to Mum over the years and he didn't seem too bad. He had also been there the day I was told about Dad, and seemed to understand that I didn't want to carry the name Baily anymore.

We all talked it over and agreed that I would use Mum and Karl's married name while I was at school. Then, if I still wanted to, they would help me change it to anything I liked before I took my exams.

School was still out for the main break, and not knowing anyone in the area I spent more time at Clare's than I did at my new home for the next couple of weeks. Sarah was often there to meet me, and then the three of us were off to play.

Sarah told me one day that Kelly had said she only hated me, and used the fact that I wasn't Dad's to wind him up to get rid of me, so; now that I was gone, things were okay at the house. Then she told me the social had stopped visiting, so I got Mum to phone them.

They told her that my case had been closed as soon as I had been rehoused, so there was no need for them to see Dad and Kelly now. I phoned them myself the following day, but they said, without evidence that Sarah had been hurt, they wouldn't do anything.

"What about what they did to me?" I shouted down the phone.

"Dave! You were beaten up at school, now you've been rehoused as you wanted, so stop making these wild accusations against your step parents please." the worker told me.

"What...!" I screamed, before slamming the phone down.

When I told Mum she said there had been a meeting a few days before. It had been agreed between them that most of what I'd told the social had happened at school; and though Dad did admit to belting me once or twice, he said he had never used a cane.

I went ballistic, screaming out all the things that had happened while kicking and punching the cupboards until one of the doors came off its hinges. Mum ran out of the kitchen to get Karl.

"Go on then, you fucking hit me and see what happens!" I screamed as he came into view, before storming off to my room.

Chapter 10
Life Without . . . Sarah

On my first day back at yet another school I was going to say that I came from the neighbouring town, but changed my mind in the end. I still didn't want to go through the real reasons why I had moved across town, but that wasn't any drama, because none of the other pupils were interested anyway. Then for the first few days I had to do a load of mock exams at the headmaster's request, to see what I had learnt so far.

I did a lot better than anyone expected, winning myself a place in most of the top classes. I regretted that later because with another change of exercise books, I was out of sync again and was soon struggling. I settled in okay though, and soon made a couple of friends.

The first few weeks I was back at school, my Aunt Daisy visited, so I would go to Clare's at the weekends and see Sarah there. One morning when I popped to the shops, I saw Kelly. I turned and walked away but she followed me, calling me every name under the sun until I ran off.

A few weeks after that, I was walking home for my lunch break from school when I saw Dad's car pull up near where I lived; then I watched as he went into my house. I hung around just up the road until he had gone again, before I went home myself.

"What did he want?" I asked Mum as I came in the back door.

"Oh, he just needed to drop a letter off for you," she replied, handing me an envelope.

Dear Mr Baily,

In light of recent events we have accepted the proposed court order on Dave.

He will no longer be allowed within one mile of your property or 500 meters of any person who resides within your household for a period of no less than five years.

We hope this meets the satisfaction of all parties involved with your case.

Yours . . .

"Yeah? So what does that mean?" I asked, not reading it.

"Well, with all the problems between you and Kelly, she doesn't want you going near the house. You're also not allowed to go near her kids either, okay?" Mum explained.

"What! What about Sarah and Clare?" I screamed.

"I'm sorry, but Clare lives too close to them, so you can't go there anymore, but you will still be able to see Sarah here," Mum answered, trying to calm me down.

"So that fat bastard can come here when he likes but I can't see my friends. Is that right? Even after what he did to me? Is that what you're saying?" I shouted back.

"He's an adult, so he has different rights to you Dave. He did say that he wouldn't try to contact you unless you wanted him too, okay?" Mum said trying to regain control.

"Fuck that, I'm going back to Clare's. They wouldn't

have let him do that to me!" I shouted, and stormed out the house.

I was still in the uniform I had to wear now, so, as soon as I got to the town centre, a police officer asked why I wasn't at school. I shrugged my shoulders and got in the back of his car to be taken home.

Mum wasn't too angry, and had already phoned the school to say I wouldn't be back that day. She tried to explain that the injunction also meant that they had to stay away from me. That was proven wrong the following week, when Dad dropped Sarah off for our visit.

I knew what time Dad was due, so I was already hiding in my room when he arrived. He came in the house and had a chat to Mum, and then I heard his footsteps coming up the stairs. The toilet was next to my room, but it was no mistake that he opened my door.

"I wanna have a chat with you Dave," he said as soon as it swung open. It was nothing to do with the way he spoke, it was just because he was there: I screamed as loud as I could until he left.

When I told Mum, she said I was making a mountain out of a molehill, and, he only opened my door by mistake. Later that afternoon I fixed a bolt to the inside of my door, so he wouldn't make the same 'mistake' again.

The next couple of times he stood outside my door talking to himself. I had my headphones on, and waited for the letter to slide under my door. Then I'd read how sorry he was, throw it in the bin and go to find Sarah. He gave up after a few weeks, but he also brought Sarah down less often.

As my thirteenth birthday came and went, I knew I was getting the present I wanted – a brand new BMX bike. And nearer Christmas than my birthday, as a joint present, I came downstairs to find the box with my new bike. It was in pieces, but I insisted I knew what I was doing and put it together myself. As soon as I was done I went out showing it off to people that didn't care.

I only got about a mile away from the house when I tried to bump up a curb. As I lifted the front wheel off the ground it fell off. I went straight over the handlebars, and I'll tell you this for nothing, the padding that was meant to protect my groin didn't help very much..., ouch! I didn't feel like riding about for a couple of days, and walked home.

The bike did give me the chance to get a paper round though. It's not that I wanted for anything: if I asked, it was bought for me; but I was rarely given any cash. And if I asked for any, I had to go through twenty questions to make sure it wasn't for the bus fare to go and see Sarah. Now, with a bit of cash or my bike for transport, I was going to see her every weekend.

I got away with it a few times and even joined her in the swimming pool for the first time. But then the police seemed to be on the lookout for me. After they had brought me home twice they said, I would be arrested for breaching my court order if I was caught again.

At school I kept few friends because I would never know what to talk about. Whenever I met someone new, they would go through their life history about this birthday and that holiday when they were nine, then ask me about mine.

The only actual birthday I remember is my tenth, three weeks after Andy died, so I'd already ran out of things to say. Again, the paper round helped, giving me enough cash to go to the local disco and have something else to talk about, but the bullies also noticed I had money.

Payday was Friday, which two fair-sized guys knew. I met them first on my way home after finishing my round. They asked me to buy them some cigarettes. I was still on my bike and just rode off. Next was an encounter at the school gates, when one of them pushed me against the wall while the other searched my pockets. I had a little bit of money with me but they didn't find it.

Then I saw them again behind the gym during lunch break. Again they pushed me against the wall, this time they told me I would have to give them fifty pence each week or I'd get the living daylights kicked out of me. A teacher saw us and called over.

I got a few more threats about what to say when the teacher got to us, then I punched the bigger of the two boys in the ear. His mate looked at me, shocked, as I ran at him, falling over as we hit. By then the teacher had arrived and took us all to the headmaster's office.

I was use to this routine and was called in first. Yes sir, no sir, and two cane strikes later I walked out.

"He can do that to me all day and I won't be bothered! See you here every Friday if you take my money! Got it?" I said to my two would-be bullies, then walked out of the reception area. They didn't bother me the following week.

Life settled after that; the bullies at school still picked on me every now and again, but as soon as they realised I was always in trouble and the teachers were watching me, they backed off. I didn't care, I was used to being in trouble.

At home there would be a lot of shouting between Mum and me. I'd nearly always demand to know who my real father was, so I could ask him to take me away. The louder I shouted, the more Mum would cry until I stormed off and stole a bottle from the off-licence.

When I got caught one day, the owner of the shop called Mum instead of the police. I insisted to her that I only drank so I didn't dream, but in all fairness I didn't even want to sleep, not with the nightmares I was having at the time.

In the nightmare I'm trapped inside my junior school classroom, within a force field of white noise. I can see the ground outside and it's shaking to the footsteps off a giant. I try to hide by ducking under the windowsill as the steps get closer. Then he's outside the window.

I become terrified and I can feel my heart beat getting faster and faster. He knows I'm there but he's waiting. Suddenly it becomes silent, and just as a great hand is coming to grab me, I wake up in a cold sweat, terrified.

When I described it to Mum, she took me to see a doctor who told me I had a condition called Post Traumatic Stress Disorder. After telling me, my condition was similar to what the soldiers coming back from the Falklands War suffered from. He went on to explain that my case was mild, with just a bit of schoolyard bulling being the cause, so, with youth on my side it wouldn't last long. Then he prescribed me some tablets to help get me back into a regular sleeping pattern.

The dreams never stopped, instead they changed and became easier to deal with. Sometimes now I'd tell Mum they were about what I thought was happening to Sarah. She would tell me that nothing was happening to her, just like nothing had happened to me.

I hated not being believed, and stopped talking about my past and became a loner, never going on daytrips or holidays with Mum and Karl. All I wanted to do was to lock myself in my bedroom, where I felt safe, and to be left alone.

I perked up about a year later when I found out Kelly had run off with her driving instructor and had moved away. I started to bunk off school so I could see Sarah again, without being caught for breaking my injunction, knowing she would've taken her kids away too. Still, it got back to Dad, and soon he was having a word with Mum and Karl about it.

When Dad came round, he said there was no need for

me to be afraid now that Kelly had gone, and that it was all her fault. Then he gets himself invited to Sunday lunch. With all of us sitting round the dining table he said, "It's so nice not having to cook for a change."

I looked up from my plate and asked, "How would you know, 'eh Sarah?"

They needn't have bothered sending me to my room; I was already on my way. Later, when they shouted for me to go and apologise, I called back that I had nothing to be sorry for. Locking myself in my own room, I didn't want an apology either; I just wanted him to go. It was bad enough him worming his way in, but before long he was best of friends with Karl.

Mum had nothing she could threaten me with when I was in trouble at school, and Karl had never tried. So, with my umpteenth letter in her hand, I wasn't worried when she said Karl wanted a word with me when he got in, for being caught smoking, again.

"I've been speaking to Jacob about you, and I think he's right," Karl said, coming in from the pub later that night. "The only thing that will work on you is the belt." He fumbled with his buckle but staggered and fell into the armchair before he got it off.

I stormed off to the kitchen and found a meat tenderiser; then, dragging a dining chair across the room on my way back, I dropped my trousers and prepared to be belted in front of him.

"Fucking try it and see what happens, you drunken bastard!" I screamed at the top of my voice. A few moments later, when nothing happened, I dressed myself and threw the chair at Karl, still slouched in the armchair.

Just before I was due to take my exams, my brother Adrian was going to get married. Inviting his real dad to his wedding sparked a new row between Mum and me about my father. She eventually told me that Adrian and

I had the same dad.

I knew the dates of previous marriages and divorces Mum had had, and they all fitted nicely. So, after another midweek wedding that I would miss because of school, I went to the reception.

"Hello, Dad," I said to the man they pointed out to me.

"Look son," he said, shaking my hand, "I've been told about this and it ain't true. I wasn't shagging your Mum at the time, someone else was, and that's why I left her. I don't know who your dad is, but it ain't me, okay?"

I held myself together until I got to the toilets, then cried for what could have been hours. Russell and Adrian found me there after they had kicked their Dad out. After that, the arguments with Mum became unbearable for the both of us, so I moved in with Adrian and his new wife.

Life there was great for a few years. I finished school, and even though I failed most of my exams, I got an apprenticeship as an engineer. I didn't finish it though, because of strike action, so I moved from job to job until I was eighteen, then followed one of my dreams and got a job as a barman.

My dream didn't last long either. The landlord of the pub I worked, and had just moved into as live-in staff, went away on holiday so a relief manager came in for a few weeks. He accused me of stealing out of the till when the landlord came back. The landlord said he didn't think I was like that, and would have given me another chance. But the complaint had reached the brewery, so he had no option but to sack me.

I had almost no friends, and just about nowhere to go; the only person willing to take me in until I could find somewhere else was Dad, and though I hated having to do it, I accepted his offer.

After I had moved the few things I had back to his

house, I walked into town to sign on the dole. Later I walked around the town centre, having a few beers, so I could face sleeping under the same roof as Dad again. It wasn't long before I'd spent my last few quid and found myself walking into an innocent-looking store.

"I want to join the Army," I said as the door closed behind me.

Life Without...

Chapter 11

"I'm Sergeant Banks, but you can call me Dean for now. Please take a seat and we'll see what we can do about that for you Dave," the guy in uniform said.

I was a little drunk, but I got the general idea of the procedure, and after a long chat, I took some forms home. The next day, I gave Mum and Dad the forms that they needed to fill out for my background checks. I was expecting trouble from them both, but I shouldn't have worried, and soon I was at my first proper interview.

"So why do you want to join the Army Dave?" Dean asked, after checking my paperwork.

"I want to get out of town," I told him, honestly.

"We'll have to come up with something better than that for the Major," he said with a chuckle.

"I need a job?" I tried.

"How's this sound?" Dean said, still with a grin on his face. "I want to learn a trade and serve my country, and in the Army I can do both."

"Okay, that'll do," I said, understanding what he meant.

"Have you had a chance to see which corps you fancy going for?" he asked.

"I've looked but I'm still not sure." I hadn't really looked.

"Well, what job do you want to do?" Dean inquired.

I thought for a few seconds. "I've always wanted to be an electrician."

"Engineers...," He wrote something down. "Anything else?"

"I like working on car engines," I said, after a bit of thought.

"REME...," He wrote that down too. "One more and we have your dream sheet mate."

"I want to make sure I get in, so, infantry." I

answered without thinking.

"To tell you the truth Dave, I think that might be a mistake for you. What are you...?" He checked his paperwork. "Fifty-one kilos: you'll struggle with all the tabbing I think. How about the Royal Signals as a Power-man? They work on generators, so you'll get the best of both worlds there, engines and electric, and best of all they're crying out for more people."

"Okay, that'll do." Anything would have done me.

Dean went on to ask a few more questions, giving me a few answers to say at my next interview. Then he sent me on my way with a training programme, details about my medical the next day, and the date and time for my interview with a Sergeant Major.

My well-rehearsed answers went down well at my second interview with the Sergeant Major, and after about an hour of chatting he said, "I'm happy enough with everything you've told me so far Mr Baily, but I'm just a little concerned about your weight. I don't know if you're aware of this, but there's a minimum weight limit of fifty kilos to join the Army and you've only just made that."

"No sir, I didn't know," I replied, thinking I'd fallen at the last hurdle.

"Tell you what I'm going to do. I'll swear you in today, but I want you to go on a PDC." He suggested, as I gave him a confused look, not having a clue what he was on about.

"Physical development course," he explained. "We normally send anyone that's overweight to make sure they can make the grade. But in your case I think it will help build you up, ready for basic training so, think of it more as a physical entrance test, okay."

"Okay sir, I'll do my best not to let you down." I started to smile knowing I was going to get away for a few weeks if nothing else.

He stood up and offered me his hand. "Good, I'll go

and see if the Major is ready to hear your oath, and let me be the first to welcome you to the British Army son. Congratulations."

Ten minutes later, after more handshakes with Dean and some instruction how to act, I was led into an office, handed a bible, and then read from a board.

"I, Dave Baily, swear by Almighty God that I will be faithful and bear true allegiance to Her Majesty Queen Elizabeth the Second, Her Heirs and Successors, and that I will as in duty bound honestly and faithfully defend Her Majesty, Her Heirs and Successors, in person, her Crown and Dignity against all enemies, and will observe and obey all orders of Her Majesty, Her Heirs and Successors, and of the Generals and Officers set over me."

After I'd finished reading, the Major passed me an envelope with twenty-seven pounds inside, my first day's pay as the Queen's Shilling, and a train warrant leaving the next day for the Midlands. Less than four weeks after moving in with Dad, I was packing again.

The next morning, I was up and out early, with Dad giving me a lift to the train station. I couldn't complain about my last few weeks with him, even though they had been awkward, so I shook his hand and thanked him for putting me up.

A few minutes later, I sat on the first of four trains. It was empty, so I took a table seat to myself and pulled out a newspaper. *Bullying in the British Army reaches an all-time high*, the headline read. I sat and read the story of an Army Barracks where the initiation of some new recruits had gone wrong and someone had got killed. I closed the paper and tried to relax, but couldn't help thinking to myself, *what have you done this time, BOY?*

"This seat taken?" some guy asked, already putting his bag on the shelf above.

I gestured that it wasn't and we had a quick introduction before Mark asked if he could have a read of my paper. He turned straight to the Army story and quietly read.

"That's a bad one," he said, putting the paper to one side once he'd finished reading. "Where you off to anyway Dave?" I answered with the name of the station I was heading for.

"Still going then, are you?" he asked.

"Yeah..., I got nowhere else to go." I replied.

As we carried on chatting I found out that Mark had been on a PDC course three months earlier, but broke his wrist on the assault course. It had happened in the last few days, but because of the injury he had to do the whole thing again to prove that it was healed.

He was average in every way, build, height, etc., and at seventeen he was two years younger than me. Telling me that he'd bummed around since leaving school, he found himself in the wrong place at the wrong time, and had got involved in drugs; joining the Army was his way of getting out of that life. My own story wasn't too different since school, having tried drink and drugs as a way to forget my past, and we got on well from the start.

It was great to arrive at the cookhouse that lunchtime knowing someone already, but looking around the full dining hall at hundreds of men twice my size, I was terrified! My hands shook so much that by the time I got to the table I'd spilt half my coffee over the floor. My nerves started to calm as other recruits were shown to nearby tables and we started to introduce ourselves as course-mates.

"Think you're going to get in this man's Army then, do you?" this monster of a bloke said as he took a seat with me and Mark.

"Fuck me, put a pack on you and you'll break," he carried on, looking straight at me. "So what do they call you then, you skinny runt?"

I turned to look at his eyes. "If you wanna have a go then let's go! Here and now! Or do you need to find some mates first?"

"You'll get jailed for fighting here you know," he replied, staring back.

"Yeah..., and so will you..., Ready?" I challenged menacingly. He got up and went to look for some mates.

"Bullied at school I take it?" Mark asked, once he was out of earshot.

I nodded in reply.

"Me too. I've got your back Dave, I know you'll be looking out for mine," he said, offering me his hand to shake. "Never seen it done like that before, but there's no doubt it works. I'll have to remember that one myself." Then we chuckled the rest of the way through lunch.

The remainder of the day was spent getting uniform issued, paperwork and a haircut, and then off to the barrack block to unpack. We were roomed alphabetically, so I was in with Mark Bradshaw and another bloke that left the next day, I didn't get his name.

That first evening was a quiet night of sorting out lockers followed by a few beers. Early the following morning we were taught some basic marching, then were off to the gym for our first physical assessment. There we had to do as many reps as we could of various exercises, sit-ups, press-ups, dips, stuff like that, followed by a timed mile run. Each exercise was marked against your age and weight to generate a score.

"Baily!" the Physical Training Instructor called.

"Staff," I answered the PTI.

"Three hundred. Excellent, not often we see a perfect score on the first attempt. Well done..., Bradshaw!"

"Staff!" Mark called, answering his name.

"Three hundred. Good to see you kept up with your training. Welcome back..., Jones!" Jones answered. "Two hundred and six. Well done mate, just a little more on your upper body and you'll be up with these two..., Davies!" And he went on through the fifty-seven of us on the course, (the guy from the cookhouse got twenty-eight by the way).

After everyone had been given their score, we were split into two groups and marched to lunch. So far, there had been no shouting or running about other than to be heard, so when the PTI ordered the group I was in to "fall out", we casually walked off to get some food.

"And you fat bastards, rabbit food! Right hand server only! Away you go!" he shouted at the group that was left. "And if I see any of you fat shits in the NAAFI bar tonight, you're out of here! Got it?"

Five or six of them walked off to the block and packed there and then. Later at dinner, as me and Mark were having a second pudding, and not feeling too sorry for the guys with mashed potato, we watched as our roommate and Lunch-boy walked out the gate in tears.

We were told that we weren't expected to reach Army standards, because, this was more an entrance test rather than full blown training. Though as a kind of introduction to Army life we still had locker and kit inspections every day. Mark had done it all before, so he taught me what I needed to know about how to do this and that, and we excelled at everything.

The fitness was easy. I suppose fighting or running from bullies half your life is good for some things, though I did sprain my ankle on a river run at the end of the first week. I'd had trouble with it since Kelly threw me down the stairs when I was about eleven, so I knew it was something that I would have to put up with; and having some bandages with me, it was fine by the following Monday morning.

During the weekend it was clear who was there to make their family proud and who was running away. Me, Mark and five other guys, out of the forty left on the course, asked if we could stay on camp while the rest went home. The troop corporal laughed when I said it was to do extra training.

Those of us left went out that Saturday afternoon, but by the evening it was just Mark and me. We talked a lot about our different reasons for not wanting to go home. No details, but let's say his childhood was as bad as mine.

The second week was a bit harder for me because we started training carrying our webbing, packed with about 5 kg; I was never far from the front though. Then I did my ankle in again on the dreaded assault course during the last day. Still, I passed with flying colours, coming second overall, beaten only by Mark.

I had thought that if I passed the course I would be allowed to stay on camp until Basic Training started. But on the last day I was given my warrant home and another to get me to Yorkshire a month later.

I really didn't want to go home, so when Mark said I could stay at his sister's for a few days, we set off together. When we got to the city that night though, we found out that she had gone away for the week and ended up sleeping rough at the station. The following day I arranged to stay with Adrian for a few weeks.

Two weeks later I was listening to the news when an item came on about an IRA shooting. Two guys who'd just finished the PDC course after mine were killed waiting at the train station. It reminded me of what I was letting myself in for, so I got back to it and got ready for Basic Training.

The last week of my leave I spent travelling. I visited Mark for a few days first, staying with his sister this time, then went to Granddad's for the last few days. He was Dad's dad, and the only person in the 'family' that didn't know I wasn't his boy.

Out of all the people in my so-called family, Granddad was a man to look up to. He was in his very late seventies when I saw him, and had worked down the coal pits of Yorkshire from the age of twelve until he was seventy-something, and he was fit!

No bigger than me when I arrived one afternoon, he took my bag off me and threw it down the hall. Then he lifted me off the floor to give me a hug and said how proud he was.

Later, when his coal delivery arrived, he was off like a shot. By the time I got to the truck to give Granddad a hand, he had two 20 kg bags of coal, one on each shoulder, and was walking back to the cellar, saying, "You've got to be quicker than that round here, Dave!"

I'm really glad I took the time to see a real man, because he died a few years later at the ripe old age of eighty-three. He looked and acted less than half that.

There was no doubt we were in the Army when we arrived the Sunday before training started and met our instructors, also known as cadre. First was Sergeant Knight; not a big man, but from day to day he was the boss, so he shouted a lot.

Next was Corporal Moore, shorter than me by an inch or two but fifteen stone of muscle. He taught weapons and tactics, and also shouted a lot.

Then Corporal Smith, not a big man compared to most, he taught field-craft and tactics, but he seemed to shout a lot too. Lastly was Corporal Brown, tall and skinny, taking us for fitness training mostly, though he shouted a lot as well..., getting the picture?

By Monday night, having been screamed at from the moment we arrived, a dozen or so would-be recruits were on their way home in tears.

"Good here ain't it?" Mark, my roommate again said, when we were finally given a break.

"Don't know what you're talking about mate, seems just like home to me," I replied, bursting into fits of laughter.

Next morning, "It's oh-five hundred hours and time for you lazy bastards to get out of bed!" shouted Smith, walking up and down the corridor banging a metal dustbin. "And what does the 'oh' mean...? Oh fuck, I'm in the Army now, is what it means. Now move it..., outside..., sports kit..., ten minutes!"

We met Brown outside for what was meant to be an eight-mile run, but it was less than three I reckon, as we did press-ups and sit-ups while we waited for the fatties to catch up. Outside the block once we were back, Brown shouted at us that we had a locker inspection next.

When we got to our rooms, they had all been done over, with beds and uniform piled in the middle of each room. After another two hours of all of them shouting at us, it was finally time for breakfast and watch another half a dozen quit.

Over the next two weeks it carried on like that, weeding out the weak and lazy. It wasn't all fitness though; the odd lesson on military history or drill was thrown in, but the shouting was constant. By the end of it there were only thirty-nine recruits left, out of seventy-two. Then it was onto basic weapons training.

"This is a ball round." Moore spoke for the first time since I had met him, as the rest of the cadre handed out what I would have called bullets back then.

"It's a seven-point-six-two millimetre, full metal jacket *live* round." He gave us a few minutes to look them over. "Hand them back to the cadre lads."

We gave them back and were handed another set of rounds that looked exactly the same, except instead of brass, these were silver in colour.

"This is a drill round, and is what you lot will be using for now..., Do not get the two confused or I will fuck you over!" he carried on as we looked at the new round.

"This," he picked up the rifle next to him, "is the L1A1 self-loading combat assault rifle, or the SLR, and was introduced into the British Army in 1954. It is a semi-automatic rifle which fires the 7.62 mm round that you have just seen, and has been used in every major conflict around the world since its introduction...," He knew his weapons, and went on for quite a while.

The next few weeks were intense with lessons, weapons, recognition of targets and the real-time situations around the world. Terry Waite was still in Beirut; there was trouble in Palestine, Iran and Iraq and with the IRA still a major player, there was a lot for us to learn.

Fitness was okay, just an hour in the gym or a five-mile run, a trot around the corner for all of us left; but the locker inspections went on hourly so we were all knackered. Then one day we had a recognition class.

"The T72 can be distinguished by its distinctive barrel, as can be seen by its'...," Sergeant Knight said at the front of the class, pointing to a picture of a tank on the wall.

"..., road wheels are evenly spaced...," was the next thing I heard after dozing off for a minute.

It was only half past ten in the morning and we were all at it. The night before, we had our last locker inspection at three, then up again at five to be ready for another one an hour later. Then it was off for a run, coming back to find the room trashed again, so thirty minutes later we were standing by our beds for another inspection before breakfast. If that wasn't enough, when we got back from the cookhouse the cadre couldn't decide what uniform we should wear.

So, with only two minutes allowed each time, we changed into every item of clothing we were allowed in our lockers. Then with another inspection due during lunch break, we ran off in woolly jumpers and jackets to a heated classroom.

"Bradshaw!" Knight shouted at the top of his voice. Everyone sat bolt upright, glad it wasn't their name that was called, as Mark shouted back, "Staff, yes Staff!"

"Aww, didn't we get enough sleepy-weepy last night?" Knight mocked. "Missing mum-zee-wum-zee, are we? You want me to tuck you in-zee-win-zee?"

"Oh, that would be great Sarg-gee warg-gee, can you read me a beddy-bye story too, please-zee wee-zee," Mark said, as calm as you like.

Half a second later, everyone including Knight was rolling about laughing. It earned us a night off, so we got to have our first beer and decent night's kip in six weeks. It got back to normal the next morning with another inspection.

It was around this time that I met Alan; as I was cleaning the spotless toilets between inspections, he walked down our lovely polished corridor with his boots on!

"I've heard there's someone from Bedfordshire in here!" he shouted as he walked past all my shocked course-mates.

I came out of the toilets and saw he was big, but I was going to be a soldier!

"Yeah..., and what the fuck do you think you're going to do about it!" I sneered as I walked up the corridor to knock him out.

"I'm from Bedfordshire too," he said, putting his

hand out. I managed to stop myself before I hit him, and shook his outstretched hand as he continued, "I'm Alan; I've been back-trooped into this one, good to meet someone from home."

I'm surprised I hadn't met Alan before; we had drunk in the same pubs, lived not too far apart at times, and were even on the same job once, though on different shifts. Even joining the Army, we reckoned we were at the same office, at the same time, on the same day, and still we had never met.

The troop he was in before would have been as bad as mine, but one of his corporals took a personal dislike to Alan. He broke his wrist in what would be labelled 'an accident'. Then Alan was held in a holding troop until he was fit enough to carry on with training.

After a shuffle around, filling up the quitters' beds, he moved in with Mark and me. He also came about the right time for me because we were moving into the combat fitness stage of training, which meant tabbing.

I hadn't had it easy by any means up to now. Army training is designed to push you beyond your limits no matter how fit or prepared you are, and the cadre, well they were good at their job; but tabbing meant carrying your pack.

My webbing, a large-pack with kit, rations, water, and extra weight for ammo, came in at 14 kg, a quarter of my bodyweight, so the big guys would rule on the tabs themselves; but the first problem was going to be packing it.

After piling the things listed onto my bed, I locked away my dress uniform and blankets, about the only things left behind in my locker.

"How the fuck!" I mouthed looking at Mark, after I put the box of rations into my inadequately named 'large pack' and half-filled it. I still had to get my sleeping bag, spare boots, waterproofs, wash kit, some gear to make a shelter with and most of my uniform into this tiny bag.

"Look." Alan gestured for us to see what he was doing. "Waterproofs…, poncho..., towel..., toothpaste..., soap and pants like this..., Bum roll like this. Got it?" We nodded as he laid the kit neatly on the floor. "Roll it as tight as you can, and...," after a bit of effort, "..., clip it closed. Right?" Mark and I nodded at each other and went to pack our own gear.

The three of us were packed in no time, with Alan showing us what he had learned in his last troop. Later that night we went round and helped the other lads who were still struggling. When Knight came up that evening to find every member of the troop, stood by their bed, packed and ready to go; he gave my room the night off, and the three of us had a beer while the others did our cleaning duties as a thank you.

With all my gear packed, I found that the weight wasn't going to be my only problem. The size of the ammo pouches meant I couldn't get my belt small enough to fit, leaving my shoulders to take the full burden. The loose belt would then rub and leave a blister all round my waist, sending me off balance as I tried to relieve the pain. That would make me stumble and soon I'd be falling behind.

Moore saw me popping one of my many blisters while we were on a march one day, and came to the block later that night. I thought I was in for it when he asked for me to take my kit to his office. When I got there though, he cut a piece of foam the size of my back, and showed me how to attach it to my webbing.

That helped to make it fit a little better, and along with Alan starting to sing as we marched, it made it a lot easier, teaching me that tabbing was all about rhythm, not speed.

A few nights later, Moore was back along with Smith

looking for a lost wallet. They lined us all up in the corridor, shouting that if it was given back within five minutes nothing else would be said or done. It wasn't back, and as luck would have it I was first in the firing line.

"You got my wallet Baily?" Moore bellowed in my ear.

I didn't have time to answer before he punched me in the stomach. It knocked the wind out of me and I collapsed to one knee.

Taking a breath, I stood back up. Thank you Staff, please may I have another?" I was breathless, but shouted pretty loud. Then Smith punched me, it hurt a lot more, so I stayed down that time.

He got through about half of us before Roberts owned up; I think to avoid being punched, as if that would have worked. He got taken to his room to return the offending wallet, and we all heard him get thrown into the lockers a few times.

"That thieving shit is gone in the morning, make sure he doesn't want to come back lads." Moore told us when he came out a few minutes later.

Half a dozen of us went to get Roberts after the cadre had left. First he was stripped of the uniform he would no longer disgrace, then he was thrown into a regimental bath that had been prepared for him.

The bathtub had as much piss and shit in it as it did water, when his clothes joined him a few minutes later. Then he was scrubbed from head to toe with the stiffest brushes we could find, before getting handcuffed to the railing outside with a plaque around his neck saying:

I AM A THIEF
PLEASE KICK
THE SHIT OUT OF ME
BEFORE I GO!!!

He didn't want to come back.

A week later; we had a couple of nights out in the field learning camouflage and battle techniques, and then we were given our first proper time off, a three-day pass with a train ticket to wherever we wanted to go.

We had learned everything we could in the classroom when the twenty-four of us remaining on the course came back from the weekend. Now it was all about honing our skills in the field, first of which was to learn how to shoot.

I was okay with my weapons drills, and had fired my rifle with a 2.2mm adaptation kit. But when a 7.62mm full metal jacket ball round leaves an SLR at 2,800 feet per second, the rifle kicks you in the shoulder like a horse on steroids! And I hit nothing.

"The skinny runt can run, but he can't shoot for shit Russ," Smith said.

"Give me ten minutes with him Smudge," Moore replied to him when he heard my score of zero.

I got back in the fire pit, and Moore adjusted the way I was holding the rifle a little. Then he stood behind me with a set of binoculars, telling me to fire off a round.

"Hmm, no need for these yet. Give me another round, Baily," Moore ordered, not bothering with the binoculars as I fired for a second time.

"Again," he said. Again I fired.

"Aim right half a target, fire." – BANG, "Up, half a target..., Fire." – BANG, Four shots later he asked, "Where are you aiming now Baily?"

"Just above target twelve, Staff," I told him.

"Give me that." He said, taking my rifle off me once I'd made it safe. Then after making a few adjustments to the sights, he handed it back.

"Your own target, fire." – BANG, "Looks about right. In your own time fire off the rest." Moore ordered.

I fired off another six rounds, and then walked the

hundred metres with Moore to see if I'd hit anything. In the centre of target eleven was the 4 by 2-inch white patch that I'd been aiming for, with seven small holes in it, each about 7.62mm's in diameter.

"Tomorrow I want to be able to cover them with a fifty pence piece Baily. Well done," Moore said, smiling.

Shooting from the squatting position was out of the question for me. Every time I fired I got pushed off balance and ended up on my arse. I got away with going into the kneeling position instead, which was by far the most comfortable position for me, and passed my weapons test with a score of fifty-eight out of sixty. Guess who beat me?

One last challenge left: the five-day, four-night test exercise incorporating everything we had learned over the last few months. With just twenty-one of us left now, we were split into three sections of seven. Smith was my Troop Corporal and split us again to dig our trenches in pairs. Once they were dug, we were off to do our night navigation test.

The following morning, after not very much sleep, my section had first aid and camouflage tests. Then the whole troop met up back at base camp, and we started to plan an ambush for that night.

It was a simple plan: we march out and hide next to a road, then wait for the enemy to pass. Once they reach the centre of our 'kill zone', we open up with everything we've got. Then after checking the pretending-to-be-dead enemy for intelligence, we run away before their reinforcements arrive.

It was pitch black and raining, but the ambush went to plan and we were moving back to our rendezvous point, when I saw the grass bank too late to do anything about it. My right foot hit the top of the bank and slipped from under me, sending me skidding to the bottom. I was still on the same foot as I hit the bottom of the bank and my ankle turned inwards ninety degrees. Hyped up from the ambush I didn't notice the pain until I reached the RV.

"What's up with you Baily?" Smith asked as I arrived in last, a rarity for me.

"Done my ankle Staff," I called back.

I took my sock and boot off so he could have a look, but he thought it wasn't too bad and let me carry on. Then we were off again, back to base camp – thankfully not too far away.

The next day my ankle was killing me, but with classroom exams that day, my section got picked up half a mile away, and dropped back off again that evening. That night we spent setting up base defences, so again not too much walking.

The last full day was another painful but easy day of filling in trenches and doing a general clean around the campsite, before the long wait for a surprise attack at two a.m. sharp. The battle was over within an hour, and after a quick debriefing we got our heads down. At around seven the next morning, Knight called us all on parade for our final orders.

"Right lads," he shouted, just loud enough for us all to hear. "It's fifteen miles back to camp from here, anyone that's not back by thirteen hundred hours has failed and will be back-trooped. Does anyone want to opt out now and get into the wagon?"

"I've hurt my back Staff," one of the lads called back. "I reckon I could make it without my webbing though."

"Okay – Baily, take Black's gear and get in the wagon." Knight ordered.

"No Staff!" I shouted back, a lot louder than I needed to.

"Baily, back of the wagon NOW!" Knight screamed.

"I can do it Staff, at least let me try!" I pleaded.

"Baily, you can't, and you'll take these two with you.

Now get in that wagon or I'll back-troop the three of you now!" He shouted, pointing in the direction of Alan and Mark, knowing they wouldn't leave me behind.

I climbed into the truck still in full battle order, with Black's kit over one shoulder to prove he'd made a mistake. Then I sat through the short drive back to camp wondering if I could face doing the last five weeks again.

I got sent to the medical centre, and then the hospital for an x-ray, but I was back in the accommodation block to congratulate the lads as they came in. With my boots off for the first time in three days, I then found I had to ask Mark if I could borrow his right trainer. He was two sizes bigger than me, but by then my foot had swollen so much that I was struggling to put socks on, let alone my own trainers.

During the last week of training, all the other lads were out practicing drill for the Pass-off Parade, leaving me in the block with nothing to do. So there I was watching TV, when Knight called me to his office to give me the news officially. So I marched in as best as I could.

"I've seen your x-ray Baily," he said as I looked down at his desk, waiting for the words *back-trooped*. "It's broken in four places..., you're not going on parade."

I looked up at him to take it like a man. *I'm getting a medical discharge; I'm out of the Army.*

"But I'm not going to make you do it again...," he continued. "You've passed. Congratulations Baily."

Even as I shook his hand I was sure I'd misheard him. "You've impressed throughout, and I almost had you down for best recruit," he carried on, standing up and walking around his desk to me. "Bradshaw got that, but believe me it was close. We wanted to give you the Best Endeavour award, but the Major put a stop to that because of your ankle. So we've had a whip round and we'd like you to accept this instead."

He took a box off his desk and handed it to me. Inside was a set of cufflinks, a tie-pin and a beautiful gold watch. Each had a single word inscribed on it.

COURAGE

I must have got something in my eye, because he handed me a tissue next.

"And might I say Baily, you're twice the soldier now than Black will ever be. Keep it up." he finished, showing me to the door.

As I walked out of his office, Mark shouted, "Hip-Hip…," and the whole troop, having snuck back in from drill practice, came out of their rooms. "Hooray!"

Then I walked down the corridor and into my own room, after being congratulated by almost everyone, to see Alan pop the cork on the champagne bottle he'd been given. I'm glad I kept the tissue, because there was definitely something in my eye now. I was a soldier!

Chapter 12

I got to watch the other lads pass off and become soldiers themselves before I was due back at the hospital. Then when the nurse showed me the damage on the x-ray, she seemed to think I'd come off a motorbike a few times without noticing.

I had broken my tibia and fibula at the base, as well as my ankle and heel bones. That was well over two weeks ago by now, so they had started to knit together out of line and would need to be re-broken. But along with that, she told me that my navicular, cuboid and all five metatarsals would need to be re-broken because of old breaks that had also set out of line.

The operation, to break just about every major bone in my foot and bolt it back to my leg, took a little over twelve hours. If you overlooked the twelve screws, three plates and about a mile of wire, it sort of looked normal on an x-ray afterwards. I walked out of hospital a week later, forgetting my crutches.

I was sent on sick leave for a couple of weeks to recover before moving onto continuation training. Then, after a few more weeks back at the Garrison, I was off to fail my driving course.

I think it was because I had only driven in stolen cars before, so when this cop car pulled up behind me during a lesson, I panicked. I was about to speed off, but my driving instructor pulled on the handbrake and the copper drove into the back of us.

The copper was fuming that I'd stopped so fast, so I told him my foot had slipped off the clutch and I'd stalled. However, in an effort to calm him down, my instructor said that he'd pulled the brake on. My instructor got three points on his licence for Dangerous Driving. I got sent back to the Garrison to do trade training.

I missed seeing Mark off to his first working unit by a week or so, but Alan was still around and we were going to be on the same trade course. And I have to say, trade training was probably the easiest thing I've ever done. There were no inspections, no guard duties, and we had every weekend off. All I needed to do was learn how to fix generators.

A generator is basically an engine that drives another part, called the generator – or in some cases, the alternator – which 'makes' electricity. I had fixed machines that built engines during my apprenticeship, so I could strip one down blindfolded. Alan had been an electrician in the real world and knew everything else. It took Mega about a week before he noticed us.

"Baily, that's got a water leak and needs a new fuel pump," said Mega 'Megaphone' Watson, our head instructor, pointing to what I knew was a 20 kW generator.

"And Alan," he went on, "there's something wrong with the alternator..., see what you can do. I'll be back in two hours to see how you're getting on." Then he left us to it.

Less than an hour later he came back and caught us with our feet up having a brew. "Well, that isn't going to get it fixed lads!" he shouted.

"Done Staff," I replied, picking up a spanner I knew I was going to need. "Just been waiting for you to take it outside, so we can run it up and bleed the system."

He told us to get on with it, and so, with a little help from Alan, two minutes later I had all the air out of the fuel system and the generator was purring like a baby kitten. We were allowed to finish our coffee before we were sent back to the lesson we'd already missed.

I would have got 100% in my final exams if I hadn't been changing a starter motor during a battery-charging lesson. I came equal second, with Alan on 98% in the end. He'd missed a full day rewiring the workshop. The guy that sat behind us in the exam got a perfect score, you work it out.

A few weeks after the course finished, there was an open day at the camp and some of us were tasked to set up the power for the beer and entertainment tents. Mega checked over some plans that he already had, and passed them to Alan and me.

It was a huge operation, so it took a few days to get everything in place ready for the tents to arrive. Mega then checked everything to make sure we hadn't forgotten anything, and we had an early night.

The first two tents arrived early the next morning and were setting up in the wrong place, so Mega went to have a word. He came back over with a piece of paper and passed it to Alan.

"How long lads?" he asked.

We had worked to a plan that had been used for years, but, for some unknown reason, the powers that be fancied a change this year and hadn't told anyone. Now we would have to re-lay every power cable on camp that we could get our hands on, about eight miles of it!

"Two days, Staff!" I guessed, while Alan nodded in agreement.

"You've got four hours..., prioritise!" Mega stated, a little worried.

Alan tore the new site layout in half. Passing one half to me he then took off across the field with some of the lads that were with us. Looking at the new plan I started barking orders at the lads left behind.

Mega went up the block and got everyone he could find, so with Mega pitching in himself when he got back, we had all the cable on the back of the trucks in record time. Now, the tents were on the move again though, so each tent got its power cable when the brass finally decided they liked that bit of grass.

Then at one minute to twelve, I heard Alan shout from a quarter of a mile away and, I tapped the sound engineer's leg. He switched his equipment on for the CO's speech at twelve-noon dead. We had three seconds to spare. A few teething problems later, Alan and I got a new plan and went to get drunk behind the NAAFI tent.

Thankfully the rest of the weekend went without a hitch. Then, on the Tuesday after checking everything we'd begged or borrowed back in, the CO called me and Alan to his office and gave us the rest of the week off.

Next we were sent to see Mega to let him know the good news. He told us there had been a whip-round the tents on the first day, and then gave us two hundred pounds. The plan had become simple..., grab the rest of the lads and get drunk!

We found as many of the lads that had helped us out as we could, and told them they had to parade at the NAAFI bar. The manager was still so thankful for all the extra work we'd put in over the weekend, all the beer was on the house. They still closed halfway through the plan, so me, Alan, and another half-dozen lads thought about town.

Walking out of a NAAFI bar on an Army training camp half-drunk wasn't the best part of our plan. Some jumped-up officer saw us and sent us to our rooms saying we were going to be charged for being Drunk in Uniform. Mega turned up ten minutes later with a minibus, laughing his head off.

"That's what I like to see," Mega he started bollocking us. "Power-men on the piss. Just get changed next time, you stupid twats. Now, get on the bus and I'll get you all out of here."

He took us to the nearest town and sat us in a pub for a late lunch. As we ate, he talked about his own time in the Army, with stories of the hard work he'd done in the Falklands and a few places I shouldn't mention. Each was followed by nights of heavy drinking and lots of women, and normally a bit of jail time for having a little too much fun.

"You're my boys," he said, "but I can only look after you so far. Now, have a good night and we'll sort the shit you get into out tomorrow." He then settled the bill.

"HI-HO!" Alan shouted. He dropped to his knees and shuffled towards the door.

"HI-HO!" I shouted, and followed suit.

"HI-HO!"

"HI-HO!"

"HI-HO!" The others followed, and Mega's boys became the Richmond Dwarfs for the night.

We shuffled into the pub next door, still on our knees, singing away. I didn't even get up when I put some money on the bar with my ID card as proof of age.

"I know I'm only a little dwarf, but could I please have eight pints of lager?" I asked the lovely barmaid. "Please, I promise they're not all for me..., Please!"

"I'll get these," Mega said, coming in behind me.

"No you won't..., they're on me," said the barmaid, pushing the money back in our direction. "Funniest thing I've seen in a long time." laughing while she poured eight pints.

"I'll pick you lot up from jail in the morning," Mega said, nodding at us before taking the minibus back to camp.

That night in Richmond went down like a storm. Every bar we went into had been warned we were coming, so by the time I'd hi-ho'd my way to the bar, there would be eight pints of lager already there, paid for by the landlord.

Then the first person to finish their pint hi-ho'd, and we would all down what drink we had left; then it was off to the next pub, shuffling on our knees, singing all the way. As some of the lads fell behind, a few other squaddies would make up the numbers and have a free drink. Then half the locals started to join in. It was fantastic.

By the time the pubs were closing, there was only me, Alan and Peter left. We sat at the bar thinking about what to do next, as I counted out how much we had left from the collection. Mega must have left his money behind at the first pub, because now I had £220.

After splitting the cash as evenly as I could, we headed for a pub we'd been told would do a lock-in if we turned up. We drank there till about three in the morning, still without spending a single penny.

Eventually we were kicked out, so we staggered to the taxi rank in the middle of town and wondered why there wasn't one waiting, four hours after the pubs had officially shut. To pass the time till one turned up, we ran around like lunatics and used a dark alley when we needed to. The police didn't see any of that, though. So with Alan wearing a traffic cone to keep his head warm, we were half asleep against a wall when they turned up.

"Three troop, I bet. ID cards, NOW!" this copper was saying as he came over.

I thought a taxi had finally turned up and headed for the back seat of his car. The other copper brought me back to the wall and asked for my ID again.

Alan was the first to come to his senses when one of the coppers knocked his hat off. He fished in his pockets, found his ID and passed it over. I was so drunk I couldn't find mine, so I emptied my pockets on the floor, and then all the notes I had blew away. I spent the next five minutes trying to collect my money back.

Peter point blank refused to get his ID out because they wouldn't give Alan his back. He was a big, strong bloke, so it took both coppers to escort him to the back of their car. When another cop car turned up a few minutes later, Alan and I just walked over and got in the back before they got out.

At the station, Alan was charged with Destruction of

Public Property, Peter with Resisting Arrest, and me with Refusing to identify myself. The RMPs must have turned up at some point, because I woke up in jail on camp, with Mega smiling down at me.

"I didn't mean it lad, but well done," he said, seeing me awake, then taking me to meet Alan and Peter, and listen to what we could remember.

A little later a couple of coppers (one of them was female by the way), turned up for our statements, Mega sat in on the interview as a character witness for me.

The male officer explained my charges, adding Drunk and Incapable before saying, "Just so you understand Mr Baily, you are still under arrest and we may need to speak to you again, so I don't want you going off anywhere." Then he turned to Mega. "Would it be possible to keep him on camp for the next couple of weeks Mr Watson?"

Bad idea!

"You're on a British Army training camp, and you know that, Constable!" replied Mega.

"You are also well aware of my rank, Constable." Mega shouted.

"Now use it! *CONSTABLE!*" There was a reason he was called Megaphone. I went deaf!

After the room stopped shaking from the seismic shock of Mega's voice, the copper apologised and asked again, with a little more respect for where he was.

I sat back in the chair and got comfy, winking at the female officer. She was cute, and I think Mega scared her a little bit. I got her phone number later, so I didn't mind the next time I was handcuffed.

"It is my understanding," said Mega at a more bearable volume, "that this man lost his ID card while I was still with him. So no, he will not be confined to camp. In fact, as soon as I get a new card sorted out for him, I will be taking him to the train station myself. Is that clear, Constable?" The copper nodded and asked if he could move on to the next one.

A couple of hours later, I was standing outside the CO's office on Orders for losing my ID. Mega went through what was going to happen: but it was just like seeing the headmaster back at school.

Yes sir – no sir – and a thank you sir later. I eventually walked out with a £50 fine and ten extra duties for drunkenness. Alan's charges were dropped, but he did do a few of my extras as a favour.

Peter was still charged with Resisting Arrest. He got a caution from the civvies and then lost a month's pay on a jumped-up Army charge of Conduct Unbecoming. We made sure he wasn't short of a quid or two though.

I'd been in the Garrison about a year now and all of my time had been spent training. I could shoot the kneecaps off a bee at some 300 metres wearing a gas mask, and I was running BFTs, (a timed one-and-a-half-mile running test), in a little over seven minutes. CFTs, (eight miles cross-country carrying full pack and rifle), I would do two in a day, just for something to do.

I knew all the training staff, and was even on first name terms with my old cadre from basic, occasionally helping them train new recruits. But if you put me in front of an audience, I clammed up and tripped over every word that came out of my mouth.

Knowing all this, of course, Alan goes and tells me he's getting married. Don't get me wrong, I was very happy for him. But my heart sank to the pit of my soul because I knew he was going to ask me to be the best man – and I was going to screw it up for him.

He edged around the subject for weeks; at one point I really thought he was going to wait until the day itself before he'd ask me, just so I couldn't back out. Then, two weeks before the wedding, he finally pulled me to one side to, 'have a quiet word.'

"Look Dave, I know what you're like, so...," *Here it*

comes, I thought. "I've asked Mark to be the best man." Alan said, then stared at me, trying to gauge my reaction.

"Thank fuck for that!" I gasped, letting out the breath I'd been holding, and gave him a manly hug.

I was to lead the Guard of Honour, the military stuff I was good at. Mega would be the photographer, and between him and Sergeant Knight they had arranged for the reception to be held at the Sergeants' Mess.

The day was fantastic of course: all of us in our blues with swords by our sides; we really did look smart. The bride looked beautiful and..., well, it was her day, so I'll leave it there.

As much as everyone had been looking forward to the wedding, I'd been looking forward to seeing Mark. He had been away at a working unit for the last seven months or so. All I had to do now was pass my driving test and I'd join him there, so I wanted to know what it was like.

He told me that at the end of the day, during peacetime, the Army was much like any normal job with a few guard duties thrown in. Keep your nose clean though and you wouldn't get too many of those.

So I took it all on board and, a few days after seeing Alan away on his honeymoon, we went our separate ways. A couple of weeks later I had finally passed my driving test, and was back in the Garrison, packing for my posting to Germany.

Chapter 13
Life Without . . . Clare

I got two weeks off before my flight to Germany, and with not much else to do after my gear had been posted on, I went to see the family. Everyone was talking to each other and it was quite a nice break – until a few days before I was due to fly out.

I was visiting Sarah at Mum's house, and as we sat in the kitchen chatting, I heard my name spoken. I didn't think much of it until I heard Clare's name and pricked up my ears. It was Karl recalling what he'd been told about her. Apparently, Clare was now some drug-crazed lunatic with two kids from different blokes.

I stormed into the living room screaming. "What the fuck did you say about Clare?"

"It's only what Jacob told me, didn't surprise me either!" he shouted back.

"And you believe that fat bastard, do you?" I screamed in his ear. "Now I don't want to hear you say another word about Clare..., got that?"

"Don't matter what I say about her now, she's dead!"

The words spun around my head and the room fell silent. I don't know how, but I picked Karl up with one hand and planted him against the wall, his feet dangling mid-air. I was going to put my fist straight through his foul-mouthed skull, but managed to hold off, throwing him to the floor instead. Then I stormed out the house, slamming the front door so hard that its pane of glass shattered behind me.

I hadn't thought about Clare in years, but I think because she'd been there through the worst of my childhood, and to hear it that way, it hit me hard. I stopped thinking and started drinking. It went on for weeks, going from bar to bar, asking everybody if they'd heard of her. No one ever had, so I started checking headstones at the cemeteries. Then, in one bar I went to, I met someone who'd known her.

"Oh, that slag...," were the last words he said before the pool cue I was holding smashed into the back of his head, and he fell asleep across the pool table.

One of his mates grabbed me from behind and the other started to punch the hell out of my face. He got a few in before I broke free and kicked him in the groin. A knee to the head later and he fell asleep on me too. The last one had his head bounced off the bar until he nodded off and fell to the floor.

"Anyone else wanna have a go!" I challenged the rest of the bar. No one fancied it, so I went and finished my pint. The police picked me up just as I was leaving.

After I sobered up, I found out three things; first I was charged with three counts of assault and looking at eighteen months. Next, I'd been AWOL for two weeks, so, along with a few other charges, I'd be looking at another seven months, and finally, Iraq had just invaded Kuwait.

I wasn't looking forward to going to jail, so I got a good solicitor and, after a short hearing he got me off on the basis I was out numbered. However, I was still fined for Public Disorder and the assaults would stay on my records. The Army was a different matter altogether. Not even Mega could shout me out of this one.

The RMPs picked me up a few hours after my hearing to take me back to the Garrison. There, I was charged with AWOL and half a dozen other things, then thrown in a cell. The following morning I was in front of the CO.

"Are you two, four..., Baily," he said in an official tone.

"Yes sir, I am."

"You are charged under section...," and he went through my charges. Absent Without Authorised Leave,

Conduct Unbecoming…, it went on for a bit.

"Do you accept my award, or elect trial by Court Martial?" he asked at the end.

"Your award, sir," I replied.

"Fifty-six days detention. RSM, take him away!" he ordered, sending me off to jail.

"And Baily!" the CO added as I was ordered to about turn. "Think yourself lucky the Brigadier didn't want you on a Court Martial. Because as far as I'm concerned; you're a coward for going AWOL when your unit is fighting in Iraq!"

I turned again and went for him, but the RSM grabbed me before I could rip his throat out for calling me a coward. Then I was frogmarched down to the gatehouse to start my now seventy-two-day sentence.

When I got to the jail I was thrown into a cell with my kit and a plan of how to lay it out on the bed. A couple of hours later, my door was unlocked and I'm told to spread-eagle against the wall. I'm then cuffed, hands and ankles, ready to be marched to the cookhouse for dinner.

I could barely walk, let alone march, so I asked politely for the ankle cuffs to be taken off. But because I was in for AWOL they were scared I'd run off. I was the fastest man in the Regiment at the time, so not one of them would have had a hope in hell of catching me if I did decide too.

I told the guard to bring my dinner to me and went back to my cell. He locked the door, but must have forgotten my order because I never got anything to eat. The same thing happened at breakfast the next morning. Felt just like home.

I'd eat most times; it just depended who was on guard that day. Some would take me to the cookhouse in the Rover, most would bring me a cold meal. But almost every time I had to leave my cell, there would be three guys waiting to cuff my wrists and ankles first.

Had a good day when Mega was Duty Sergeant. He took me down the pub for a couple in the evening. The Duty Officer went ballistic and said he would get Mega busted, but he managed to shout his way out of it, as usual.

Had some bad days too, the worst being some jumped-up corporal doing Guard Commander. He got the lads on duty to bang on my door, calling me a coward, all through the night. I was waiting for him behind my door next morning. I broke his nose as soon as it opened. Then I was told I'd get no time off for good behaviour.

The worst thing in jail though was the boredom. All day every day, locked in a six-by-eight room with only a bed and a chair, waiting for someone to shout at me – seem to remind you of anything?

Then, with lights out at eight, the only thing left to do was to think. I'd think about how I'd just thrown away my Army career. Think about Clare, and how she might have died. And think about the childhood she'd helped me through, then remember what I went through. Then to be called a coward. I hated it!

After seventy-two days of near solitary confinement, I was carried up a set of stairs to be released from jail by the camp Adjutant. But things didn't get much better when I landed in Germany, over three months later than expected.

I was told that someone would pick me up at the airport, but when I landed in Germany there was no one about. I hadn't been given a phone number and I didn't have a clue where the camp was, so I got in a taxi and just said, "Army camp." But because I couldn't speak a word of German, the driver ends up taking me to the wrong camp. Then after having paid the fare I was out of cash, so I had to ask for transport to the right camp.

I got a bollocking for going to the wrong camp and asking in the first place; and when I arrived where I should have been, I got another bollocking for not phoning for them to pick me up.

That was followed by yet another bollocking from my new troop Sergeant for being a day late. He warned me for Orders and took me to meet the Sergeant Major for another bollocking, and then I'm off to see the OC Squadron. He reads out my charge of 'Absent from Place of Duty' and I'm back to jail for another seven days. Don't know how they worked that out; I'd only been released that morning!

I met Mark on my second day inside, and he told me the Regiment had it in for me. They had just come back from Iraq and thought I'd gone AWOL to get out of going. I started to think, *what have you done this time, BOY?*

So, about four months after getting my dream posting and spending most of my time in jail, I finally got to meet my new roommates. Glen was the first, and I was glad of that. He was a genuine bloke and the first person to ask why I'd gone AWOL. He understood and we got on well. Tom was a bit of an arse, but I could understand why, we got on most of the time.

Glen helped me pick up the kit I'd posted months before. It had all been neatly packed in three wooden boxes, and when we got them off the shelf I found all the lids had been broken into. QM, the boss down there, didn't care. It happened before they got there apparently. The bastards had nicked my watch.

Then while I'm unpacking later that day, the Sergeant Major decided to have a room inspection. I had locker inspections every hour after that till midnight because I hadn't been ready for it. I was glad I was in Germany, where the pubs were open twenty-four hours a day, if you knew where to go. And Mark knew where to go, because he wasn't having a good time either.

He was working in the stores when everyone went to

Iraq. But when the Regiment moved forward over the border he stayed behind in Saudi Arabia. As far as the guys in the Regiment were concerned, if you weren't good enough to go to war with them, you weren't good enough to be with them now.

That seemed to put me in trouble for everything. Kit not ironed well enough. Anyone else would have got a re-inspection; I got change parades all night. Boots not polished when coming off guard duty. Anyone else would get a bollocking; I would get five extra duties.

Once, I was ordered to move a vehicle five feet. I got a £250 fine and fourteen days Restriction of Privileges for not putting a seat belt on. There wasn't even a seat belt fitted in the bloody thing, for God's sake!

I didn't get on at work either. The Corporal above me thought I didn't know enough about generators to work for him. Even after I'd shown Glen how to un-seize an engine, it still wasn't good enough. I got side-lined into the stores in the end. That was fine by me though, because now I could get all the kit I needed for RoP's.

It was like basic training all over again, but at least you could pass that. Here, I didn't stand a chance, so it was leave or get kicked out. Only problem was, I'd signed up for six years and it would be another twelve months before I could even buy myself out.

I didn't bother booking leave over the Christmas holidays because, I already knew I'd be getting extra duties. Then, sure enough, on New Year's Eve, me along with all the other bad boys on camp are taking it in turns to stand at the gate for two hours at a time, and I pull the last stag. On New Year's morning, about a quarter of an hour after I should have been relieved, I bang on the window asking where the next guy was.

"Shut up Baily! You're on first stag!" the Guard Commander shouted back.

Two hours later I'm finally relieved, and get a chance

to explain that I've been there since the day before. Someone checks the roll to make sure, and finds out he's three guys short. Two were found in the block with hangovers, and I had to replace the missing third guy.

They sent me on an easy duty, granted, just two of us up at a storage depot about ten miles from the main camp. But my Guard IC was one of the guys with a hangover, and went straight to bed when we got there.

So I sat at the front desk, my instructions being to phone the main camp every hour. I managed two calls before my IC woke me up with the phone ringing off the hook. Then I listened as he told them how he had just come in from a perimeter check and found me asleep, before he passed me the phone.

The guy on the other end shouted for a few minutes, telling me that I would be warned for orders when I got back, and to make sure I didn't fall asleep again, I was also to be out on patrol every half hour for the rest of the duty. As I slammed the phone down, my IC was already backing away with his hands in the air.

"It'll be alright mate," he was pleading. "They'll calm down when I tell them you were on duty last night. Nothing will happen to you."

"Yeah, right!" I shouted back at him. "With my record I'll be doing twenty-eight days, you fucker!"

"Honest, I'll sort it. I know the Duty Sergeant. It's okay mate." He tried to reassure me.

"You'd better!" I threatened, taking my rifle out of the rack and picking up a magazine with ten live rounds. "Because now I've got to carry a gun. Want to watch me load it?"

He didn't, so I walked around the perimeter fence after that, and every few minutes I would give it a kick. That would have sent the alarm panels in both guardrooms crazy, but they would know I was awake. About an hour later I went back and saw my IC beckoning me to go in.

"Got one up the spout, have you?" he asked, seeing that I hadn't taken the magazine off my rifle.

"Wanna play chicken and find out?" I dared, staring him out.

"You're making me nervous, especially with what I've got to tell you. So please?" he begged, holding out his hand.

I took the magazine off and handed it to him. He stood looking at it for a few moments before unloading the ten rounds I had gone out with.

"I ain't gonna kill you. But I might beat the shit out of you if you don't give me some good news," I said, taking a seat.

"Look," he replied. "I've written it up in the book that I've already disciplined you with extra details, so nothing more will be said about it, okay? It's about the best I can do." He said, and started to relax a little.

"Right, I get to walk about again all night so you don't drop yourself in the shit! Don't get too close to me," I shouted, and went back on patrol.

A few hours later my Sergeant Major, the Duty Officer that day, turned up at the depot. He was adamant that the extra patrols I was doing were only part of my normal duty and wanted me on charges. My IC gave in and I was warned for Orders.

I wanted to be alone after that, so I spent most of my time walking round the depot or standing at the gate. At around three the following morning, while I'm stood at the gate, I noticed a car a few hundred metres down the road.

I really didn't think much of it at first, but as the minutes ticked by it seemed to be edging closer. Then the high beams came on, blinding me for a few seconds and hiding the car in a plume of smoke from now screeching tyres. By the time I could make the car out again, it was on top of me. Then everything seemed to happen at once, but in slow motion.

From the passenger side of the car I saw a flash and heard the bang of a gunshot. I bolted off, cutting across at an angle towards the road. As I ran, I cocked my rifle and counted another four shots from the car. Before I knew it, I was standing in the middle of the road and aiming at the back of the car as it sped away.

As I fired my first shot, I was already dropping to a kneeling position. I was sure I saw the rear window shatter; so, adjusting my aim just a little, I fired off another two rounds. The car swerved across the road and out of sight. I chased after it, but it had gone by the time I got to the corner.

"Zero, this is Alpha-Delta – Contact – Wait out!" I called into the radio.

Suddenly, it came alive with chatter asking me to repeat what I'd said. I called back again, adding some code words to say that this was the real thing.

"What the fuck have you done now?" my IC asked, handing me the phone when I got back, then I watched the colour drain from his face as I went through the incident.

The guy I was speaking to on the phone didn't have a clue what to do. First, he told me to wait where I was until he could get hold of the Duty Officer. A few minutes later, he phoned back telling me to get back on the gate and wait for someone to turn up.

I grabbed my gear and took up my position at the front gate, looking out for headlights, hoping I would be able to tell the difference between one of our Rovers, or the car coming back for a second try. A few minutes later, a dozen lads got out the back of a truck, and within minutes the area was secured. Then I was taken back to camp to write my statement.

I was confined to camp while the investigation went on. Every few days someone would want to re-check the endless details of what had happened, and would call for me. After a few weeks my Sergeant Major eventually marched me into the CO's office to hear the outcome.

The car with the gun had been found about a mile from the depot. All three of my shots had hit the car – the first shattered the back window as I thought, the other two went through the boot and car itself to be found in the engine compartment – but the suspects had got away. Then the CO congratulated me for my actions and lifted all the restrictions I was under.

I should have been looking forward to celebrating, but outside the CO's office I handed my beret to my Sergeant Major, and was marched back in on Orders. The CO read out my name, rank and number without looking up from his desk. Then he moved on to my charge of Sleeping on Duty, before he realised I was standing in front of him again.

"What is going on with you Baily?" he shouted. "First I'm writing up a commendation, and then you're back in here on Orders for Sleeping on Duty. Have you got anything to say before I pass judgement?"

"Sir, I had been on duty the previous day also," I offered in my defence.

"What do you mean? The previous day?" he asked.

"Sir, I reported for duty at oh-seven hundred on New Year's Eve and was not relieved until after the incident on the morning of the second, sir," I explained.

"Is this true Sergeant Major?" the CO asked, turning his head.

"The Guard of that day was undermanned, sir," the Sergeant Major replied. "Baily was detailed to make up the number until a replacement could be found, sir."

"But, if I'm getting this right, that wasn't until four the following morning. Am I right?" the CO checked.

"It is my understanding that no one could be found, sir," explained the Sergeant Major.

"Baily," the CO turned back to me, "you have heard the Sergeant Major's comments. Do you have anything to add?"

"Yes sir," I answered. "I believe I have already been punished for the offence, in that, I was given extra guard patrols to carry out by the guard IC of the depot, sir."

"So, let me get this straight. You were found asleep on the second day of your duty, not the first. Correct?" the CO asked.

"Sir," I agreed with a nod.

"Then, you were given extra patrols?" the CO seemed to want to know more detail.

"A thirty minute patrol every hour, for the rest of the duty, sir," I filled in.

"Then you are involved in the drive-by shooting at oh-three hundred'ish. Right?" he checked.

"Yes sir, that's correct." I confirmed.

The CO took a moment to ponder. "Sergeant Major, give this soldier his beret back!" he scowled, glaring at the Sergeant Major before turning back to me. "I'm going to see if I can get you a Mention in Dispatches. So hold your head up high when you leave here son."

I had been charged eighteen times over the previous six months and had spent at least four weeks of that time in jail, so I didn't get the Mention. But a Brigadier's Commendation and a mention in a forces magazine was enough to stop people calling me a coward, and life got a little better in the Regiment for a while.

Chapter 14
Life Without . . . Mark

Life for me in the Regiment may have got better, but Mark was still having a hard time and was planning to buy himself out. I talked him into holding off for a few months, because I'd decided the Army wasn't for me either. Then we started to make plans to get a house together once we were back in the UK, but nothing definite. We were just waiting for the date when I could sign off too.

For the most part, the few remaining months I would've had left, I was bored. I was still working in the stores but they were only open for two hours per day. The rest of my time I had to sit in an office waiting for the phone to ring. Then one day my troop Sergeant, Zed Foster, called to say I had to go out with the troop for a Saint George's Day party that evening.

I turned up at the NAAFI bar on camp at the appointed time, finding the whole regiment already drinking to the health of our patron saint. Then, a few hours into the celebrations, things started to get a bit rowdy.

Apparently it happened every year, and soon the fighting would start between the different squadrons. Mark could see the tension rising too. So while it was still quite early we left, leaving everyone else to get black eyes, if that was what they wanted.

Back in Mark's room, we carried on our more sombre celebration with a few cans and computer games. Through the evening we were joined by a couple of mates, and went on into the early hours of the morning.

By the time the beer ran out there were only four of us left, and at this stage I want to make a few things clear. We were all very drunk, and classed as bad boys by the Regiment. We all had plans of leaving the Army as soon as we could. And we all had a history of using drugs *before* we joined up. And, we all agreed to take a hit off the bottle of gas when it appeared in the room.

The high that gave me was instant, and I fell back in a trance-like state. Time didn't matter anymore. Even the fly buzzing around the room seemed to slow down. It could have been seconds, or, quite as easily weeks before I watched Mark take a second hit. The bottle, slowly, sliding from his hands to hit the floor. Then he kicked a chair over and poleaxed onto his bed.

"Too much for you?" someone slurred. And Mark started to have a fit.

My senses came back and I dived for him, holding his shoulders down as he thrashed about. A few seconds later, he stopped. I felt his neck, then put my ear to his chest, but I couldn't hear anything.

"Fucking help!" I shouted, and started to pound rhythmically on Mark's chest. One of the other lads took over the breathing duties, and, together we tried to save his life.

We failed.

The other two lads dragged me off Mark and pulled me to their room. After they had calmed me down, I eventually agreed not to drop them in it by saying anything until Mark had been found officially. By then it was morning, and I was due at work; so for the whole day I just locked myself in the stores crying, hoping I wouldn't break my word while I waited for the news. By the time I handed the keys back I'd still heard nothing.

I went back to Mark's room that night to keep him company, trying to think of what to do next. Then, well into the following morning, I signed the keys out for the stores again. In the office, I picked up the phone and dialled the Officers' Mess, where Mark had worked.

"This is Major Babcock in room twenty," I said in a posh voice. "Send the boy up to collect my shoes will you my good man." Then I hung up the phone.

When I took the store keys back to the Guardroom, they were already dropping the flags to half-mast. I was sent to cell two to be told that they'd found him.

I was held in the cells on suicide watch, and because of the gas bottle they'd found, a drugs investigation started. That brought the Special Investigation Branch, (the military equivalent of CID) to camp; so after they had fingerprinted the room, the questioning started.

They knew there had been more than one person in the room when Mark died, and I was a prime suspect to be one of them, of course, though I was trying to deny I was involved. Then they went on about how dangerous this gas was, telling me in graphic detail how it killed instantly.

"We know you were in the room," said one of the SIB officers. "All we need to know Baily, is who the others were. We need to tell them how dangerous this stuff is. Don't you understand that?"

"How do you know I was there?" I demanded.

"We've got your fingerprints over everything. So admit it will you?" he shouted and threw a few sheets of paper across the table. Apparently the black smudges were my prints making this the evidence they had against me.

"Have you checked my room? You'll find Mark's fingerprints everywhere! Does that mean he was there last night?" I screamed back, and started crying.

I was released three weeks later without charge after passing two drugs tests. The other two lads went AWOL. I heard one of them did five months when he was caught.

Mark's death had been classed as accidental suicide, so when his family asked, they said he could have a military funeral. Thankfully for me, when I got out of jail there was still a few days to go before the ceremony, so I went to meet Mark's troop Sergeant to ask permission to go.

He said that the only way I could was if I was a pallbearer. But I knew Mark's final wishes, just as he'd known mine, so, I adamantly refused. Then the Sergeant threatened that I wouldn't be allowed to go to the funeral at all; but I made it all the same.

After the ceremony, and being off camp for the first time in a while, I took some time off. I was caught five days later, when the German friends I'd been staying with called the RMPs. I hadn't stopped crying the whole time I had stayed with them. Sentenced to twenty-one days for AWOL, I spent a lot of time crying there as well.

As I came to terms with everything, I tried again to follow Mark's wishes and let him go, so I could get on with life. It would've been extremely hard staying on the same camp day after day, so I asked for a posting. It was quickly approved, but it would still be two months before I was moved.

I was released from jail a week early for good behaviour. Then I was moved into the transport department to wait for my paperwork to go through. A few days later, there was hardly anybody on camp as the Regiment got sent out on a field exercise.

I was to stay on camp carrying out rear details and was one of the few drivers left on camp. Then reporting to Zed I was given my first detail of the day: to the crematorium, where Mark's funeral had been a few weeks before.

I pleaded for him to send someone else, but then Zed said the order had come direct from the Sergeant Major, and I had to go. After he added that Mark's remains were already with his family, I reluctantly set off.

When I got to the crematorium, this German bloke came running out with a cardboard box, shouting

"Hanover!" and the time I had to be there. I should have guessed by the address and gone straight back to camp, but it didn't register until I pulled up in Hanover hours later. There I saw a sign saying 'The Royal Signals Cemetery', and opened the plain box at my side.

There were a number of reasons why I took Mark's ashes back to camp, but the main one was, in his Last Will and Testament, he had stated where they should be scattered. And I was going to see that was done.

I did have a really rough time with my emotions on the drive back; but, wanting to get Mark home, I kept control. Then in the middle of the night I arrived back at camp and was sent to see my Sergeant Major.

He was in an office that was being used as a command centre for the regimental exercise, sitting at a radio, when I stormed in.

"You fucking knew, didn't you?" I screamed at the top of my voice.

"Yeah, I did!" he shouted back over his shoulder. "Now where is the lazy bastard so I can charge him for being late for his own funeral?" Then he laughed at his joke.

I went out to the Rover and drove it up into the doors of the building, running off with Mark's urn. Before I made it off camp, some bloke rugby tackled me, then a few of his mates jumped on top of us, and I was carried off to the cells.

A little later, the Sergeant Major turned up at my cell door shouting that he considered I was Refusing to Soldier, adding, he was going to make my life hell for as long as he could. An hour later, he had four or five guys join him with orders to strip my cell. I put up a fight to keep the urn, but was left with only my boxer shorts for dignity. Every few hours after that, someone would open the door just to have a go at me.

I got told it was four days before my Sergeant Major

came back to the cells. By then, I was refusing to even speak until they kicked me out of the Army. He opened the door and started his rant about how worthless I was, and then poked me with his pace-stick.

"What's up with you Baily? Didn't your daddy beat you enough when you was a kid!" he shouted.

I looked at him, but it was no longer my Sergeant Major I was seeing: it was Dad standing there. And this wasn't just about Mark; every bad memory I had was running through my mind.

I grabbed the end of his pace-stick and snatched it out of his hand. Standing up, I spun full circle and brought it down on his head as hard as I could. I don't think he felt the second blow.

Unconscious, he was dragged out by his feet. Moments later, my cell was filled with guards fighting to put hand and ankle cuffs on me. Two of them joined the Sergeant Major at the hospital to get stitched up.

Because of the light outside my cell window, it was difficult to judge time. A plate of food would arrive, and sometimes I'd get to eat it before it was taken away. Also, I found that if I banged on the door for long enough, I would be allowed to use the toilet. Other than that, I rarely saw anybody, until one day the Padre turned up in uniform.

"Hello Dave, is it alright if I come in?" he asked politely at the door.

Other than a few obscenities, I hadn't said a word to anyone in over two weeks by my reckoning. And I knew that if I could hold out for a few more, I'd be kicked out of the Army for Refusing to Soldier. So I looked at his rank of Colonel, then back at the floor, without saying a word. He came in anyway and asked permission again before he sat on the bed frame and started talking.

Then he told me about his dog and cat having a fight, and he told me his shopping list for the week. It seemed to go on for hours as I found out his wife was a little under the weather, nothing serious, just the flu he thought. He talked and I listened. Then he thanked a guard for passing him a bag of food, and turned to me before he said, "Eat. There'll be more tomorrow." Then he left.

Later that night, two guards held me against the wall while another one put a mattress, duvet and a pillow on the wooden bed frame.

"That looks a little comfier," the Padre said the next time I saw him. "Mind if I try it out?"

I looked up and nodded.

"Good. Perhaps now you know I'm not your enemy we can get started. Now, is there anything else I can do for you Dave?" he asked, as he settled on the end of the bed.

I lifted my hands to show him the cuffs.

"I'm sorry Dave," he replied apologetically, "but these are serious charges against you, so the cuffs are there for my protection. But I'm sure I can get them loosened if that would help?"

"When I'm asleep, they hurt," I told him.

The Padre called for the key to be brought to him and took the cuffs off. The relief when the sensation came back to my hands and feet was intense. I lay back, and while listening to the Padre talking about his daughter's riding lesson, I fell asleep. I woke up some time later to find a bag with a note in it reading, "Eat there will be more tomorrow."

The next day, the Padre was a good few hours into talking about nothing when I asked him how long I'd been in jail for.

"Nineteen days Dave, only another nine to go, and then I won't be able to help you. Ready to talk yet?" he replied.

"Leave the uniform at home and I'll think about it," I said with a smile.

He smiled back. "Bit silly of me, really," he said. "I'm not going to jeopardise your Refusal to Soldier, though I would be your Defending Officer if you change your mind. Until then, I can still help you with your defence because; well I'm not sure if you know this but, when you do get released you'll be handed over to the civilian police and charged with assault with a weapon. I'll try harder tomorrow, but you must too, okay? Now eat…,"

"There'll be more tomorrow. I promise," I finished off for him.

We talked a lot the following day about the endless military charges I would be facing, ranging from Resisting Arrest to Destruction of Army Property and multiple Assaults. It would have meant up to six years, with a dishonourable discharge. My best option was to continue to Refuse to Soldier. Then under armed guard, I'd be taken back to the UK to be charged. There I could get up to around twelve months, but the military charges would be dropped on my discharge.

"So Dave, it looks like we need to concentrate on these assaults so, I'll have to ask you this first. Was there any reason why you acted the way you did?" the Padre asked the following day, now dressed in a tracksuit.

"He said he wanted to be my Dad," I told him coldly.

"Oh, and why should that be such a bad thing?" he asked, tipping his head.

"You ever met my Dad?" I shouted. Obviously he hadn't, so I filled in a few details. "He is a fat, lazy bastard that beat the shit out of me when I was a kid. Now, if that man wants to be like that, he deserves everything he got!"

"I see Dave, there's a lot of hatred there. Do you want to talk about it?" the Padre asked, with more than a little concern. As I shook my head he continued. "Well, if you're not going to talk about it, we can't use it in your defence."

"I hit him, so I'm guilty," I screamed. "I'll do whatever time they give me and start again." I folded my arms, really not caring how much time I was going to do in jail.

"Do you want to spend the next year in a room like this?" the Padre gestured around my virtually empty cell to demonstrate his point.

"I don't care, it's just another shitty room to me, but at least in hear I can hear them coming, so I'll be better off." I stated, knowing they were never going to let me out anyway.

"Who? Your Dad, well, he'll have to ask permission, and even then you can still refuse visitors you know." He said in an attempt to calm me down.

"Ha! That fat bastard won't come within twenty feet of me. He knows what will happen if he does, and now so does every other fucker, don't they?" I shouted loud enough so the guards outside my cell could hear.

The Padre tried a new tactic and stayed quiet for a few minutes, allowing me to calm down, before he tried again,

"Is that why you haven't asked about him yet?" he said eventually.

"His sister picked him up, so he's gone home," I said in a whisper.

"No Dave, he's still in hospital." There was another moment's pause, as he seemed to be thinking about something. "Oh, you're talking about the young lad's ashes, Yes, I believe the family have them now." he finished gently.

"His name is Mark, okay?" I stated rather too loudly.

"Did you know the lad – I mean Mark?" the Padre asked, leaning closer.

"I joined the fucking Army with him! Of course I did! He was my best mate for gods' sake!" I screamed, before bursting into tears.

He gave me the time I needed to compose myself before we started again. This time with the reasons I was in jail in the first place. I calmed down a bit as I recalled my time in the Army so far, and listing everything I'd been in trouble for. By the time I'd finished, we had the basis of a defence.

All I had to do was convince a judge that I'd been bullied to breaking point. With my outstanding record from training, along with a Brigadier's Commendation, and yet charged so many times by one man, it should be easy enough.

About the only thing against me now were the assaults I'd been charged with back when I was told Clare had died. That would probably mean about three months in a civilian jail. But, with time served while Refusing to Soldier taken into consideration, effectively I could walk free.

The Padre only popped in for a few minutes the following day, dropping off a bag of food and his, "Eat, there'll be more tomorrow" line – I guess it must have been a Sunday. Then, over the next few days, he gathered the statements and the evidence I'd need to give to my solicitor when I was handed over.

"So, how is the Sergeant Major?" I asked one day, as the Padre was reading one of the guard's statements from the night of the assault.

"Didn't think you cared Dave," he answered, looking up.

"I don't, but you were going to tell me the other day. Has he been let out of hospital yet?" I asked quietly.

"I'm afraid not, you hit him pretty hard, fracturing his skull. Then there were a few complications that meant he lost his hearing and the sight from one eye. How does that make you feel?" he asked sombrely.

Shrugging my shoulders, I felt guilty at how bad the Sergeant Major was, but then I thought of the man I saw standing in the cell doorway that night. He was a lucky man really; I would've killed him.

"Suppose his family want to see me go down forever, don't they?" I said softly, looking at the floor.

"His wife's angry of course. But she understands that there are reasons why you did what you did, so no, not really. In fact she said to tell you that she doesn't want to see you throw your life away over it. Shall we carry on?" he replied, and continued reading from the statement.

A few days later, the news that my Refusal to Soldier would be accepted came through. In just a few hours after the final paperwork had been signed off, I would be free of all obligations to the Army. And by the end of the week a judge would decide if I had paid enough for my crimes or not. So while taking a shower, I began to think seriously about my future for the first time. Where would I live? What job? Girlfriend?

I heard the Padre call for me, but it was another ten minutes before I walked into the Provo's office, stark naked and still dripping from the shower.

"What do I have to do to stay in the Army?" I asked.

"Are you sure Dave?" the Padre said, questioning me with his look.

I nodded.

"It could mean a long time in jail for you." He warned.

I nodded.

"Well, if we're going to do this, we're going to do it right. So I'll be doing my best to get you to soldier on after your sentence, okay? Now, all you need to do is follow an order." The Padre said, smiling at me.

I braced up to attention. "Sir, I am yours to command, sir!" I shouted at the top of my voice so that everyone on camp could hear me.

"Then my first command to you young soldier, is put some damned clothes on. It's embarrassing having you stood in front of me like that," the Padre ordered, and burst out laughing as he pointed to a bag in the corner.

There was still the matter of all the charges against me, and after getting new uniform issued, the CO officially warned me for Court Martial, before I was marched back to jail under close arrest.

We continued with my defence of being bullied, and when it was presented to the tribunal they dropped over half the charges. The Court Martial was dropped, and so it fell to the Garrison Commander, (the same person that awarded my commendation), to hear the charges against me.

Striking a Senior Non-Commissioned Officer –
Fifty-six days and soldier on.
Two counts of striking Other Rank Soldiers –
Fifty-six days and soldier on.
Destruction of Army Property –
Twenty-eight days and soldier on.
Refusal to follow Orders –
Twenty-seven days and soldier on.

One day more and it would have been compulsory for me to go to Colchester. As it turned out, I would be spending the next six months in various camp jails around Germany.

The Sergeant Major did get his hearing back by the way. Then when he left hospital he was ordered to take early retirement or face Court Martial himself. He took retirement so that he could keep his pension. I'm okay with that because, his family shouldn't have to suffer for what I did to him.

My first stint inside was meant to be four weeks with the Coldstream Guards, but it didn't start too well. The Provo, (sort of like a jail warden), didn't like scrawny little shits that beat up defenceless Sergeant Majors, so he was going to teach me some respect, like my Dad should have.

I told him what happened to the last man who wanted

to be my Dad. Then I got him to picture what *this* scrawny little shit would do to him if he tried. The Padre picked me up the following morning and took me to the Paras' jailhouse instead.

On the way, we laughed about why I had been kicked out of jail, a first for the Padre. Then he said something that has stayed with me ever since.

"I get to meet a lot of people like you in my line of work, you know," he was saying gently, with the caring-Padre side of him coming through strong. "People that have a troubled mind yet can't find a way to talk about it. Most of them bottle up all the bad things until they burst, much like your situation I think?"

He had hit the nail on the head, and I nodded in agreement.

"Well, there are people out there who rather than talk to someone, they write about it, and they find it helps them to cope. They say it's like talking without speaking. Then, if you still don't want other people to know…, well, there's always the bin, so no one will ever read it if you don't want them to." He finished his story.

We had another laugh about how I'd hardly been at school because I was always suspended for fighting; then I failed most of my exams, so I could barely write a full sentence, let alone the book I'd need to. But I agreed to give it a go anyway. If nothing else, it would give me something to think about for the next six months.

The Paras' Provo had been told not to mention my Dad before I arrived, so I settled in a little better there. It was hard time though, starting early each morning with a log run, and only the good Lord himself could have kept count of how many times I went over their assault course.

Next, I was with the Dragoons for a few weeks of polishing everyone's boots and drill – boring, but an easy time really. Then I was mucked about by the

Signals for a month. But I was settling into jail life by then, so I got on with it until I eventually headed off to the Artillery.

Now they know how to jail people, I can tell you. I was introduced to my cellmate on the first day – a 40 lb. Artillery cartridge – and I had to do everything for it. I had to clean the floor, for the cartridge. I had to shower, the cartridge. I had to read bed time stories to, the cartridge, and I'd have to march the cartridge to meals. I even had to write the cartridge a Dear John letter when I left. I miss my cartridge.

The Dragoons asked me to pop back after that because they had a parade coming up. And finally, after a few weeks of polishing yet more boots, belts and swords, the Padre picked me up and took me to my last jail.

We stopped on the way for a break, and as we ate the Padre asked about the A4 pad I had begun to keep with me. I had no problem with passing it over when he asked, and after he had read all my love letters to My Darling Cartridge, he came to a page that had just two words written on it: *Life Without...*, He looked up.

"Don't know where to start," I said, a little dejected.

"You have my boy. You already have." He replied softly.

Chapter 15

My last stay in jail was also to be my new working unit once I was released, so the first job on the cards was to pick up my personal gear from the stores. Then, leaving it still packed in boxes in what would become my new room, I was escorted back to the cells to sort out my military kit.

The guard that day didn't seem to be expecting me, but after a few calls the Guard Commander decided to take responsibility of me, and I saw the Padre off for what would be the last time.

Each jail had its own routine, so I asked a few times when my next inspection would be. Again they didn't seem to know anything, so I started polishing a pair of boots that I'd found, no doubt left by the Provo as a welcoming present. After a few hours I've gently brought the boots up to perfection, and waited for lights out.

"You got combats with you?" the Guard Commander shouted down the corridor.

"I'm in jail. I've got everything with me," I shouted back.

"Good, because I'm two men down, so you're on stag in ten minutes. Now get changed!" he hollered, and went back to the front desk.

Thinking he wasn't serious or that maybe it was an inspection, I got changed. But sure enough, ten minutes later he was dragging me to the front desk. Someone then dumped a flak jacket over my shoulders and gave me a rifle with ten rounds.

"Sign here," he ordered, and I'm told to load the rifle myself because he didn't have the time. I went outside and put the magazine on the rifle. Then I spent my first night in that jail doing guard duty, thinking, *wait till the Padre hears about this one.*

I was enjoying the freedom and the fresh air, so I volunteered for extra turns at the gate. As people started to arrive for work in the morning, I asked some Sergeant for his ID – but how was I to know he was the Provo?

After a lot of shouting he warned me for Orders for not knowing who he was. Then the shouting started in the Guardroom a few minutes later, as he discovered he was missing a prisoner, before the window opened.

"You going to run off on me Baily?" Dinger shouted across.

"Wouldn't dream of it, Staff. It's been quite enjoyable so far," I shouted back, laughing.

Dinger wasn't your typical jailer. He had refused to soldier himself, and then changed his mind. He got a bit of time for his crime, as I did, but soon found himself shooting up the ranks. Because of our similar history, and with the almighty cock-up the night before, we became friends ten minutes later while I was making coffee.

"You do these Baily?" Dinger asked, putting the boots I'd polished on his desk.

"Yes Staff." I told him, sorting out the cups.

"I was going to throw them out, but now hmmm…, so I bet if I checked your cell I wouldn't find a thing out of place?" Dinger wagered.

"I wasn't given a layout plan Staff, so I laid it out like the Dragoons," I replied. "I still have their plan, if you'd like to check." Then I started digging in my pocket for the sheet of paper, thinking it would be a good starting point for this jail.

"Yeah, I recognise it," he said with a snigger. "I'll see if I can get you out early mate, but the CO here is a twat, so it probably won't happen. But until you do get out, I'll make sure no one mucks you about, okay."

I got released two weeks early for good behaviour and moved to a holding squadron. Army cutbacks were going on at the time, so there wasn't much to do other than paint vehicles endlessly. I stayed out of trouble though, and settled into normal Army life for the first time.

A few months went by, and then there was a shuffle-about into the new slim-line unit we had become, so I was moved to a new squadron. As I walked into my new Staff Sergeant's office, I saw Zed Foster, my old troop Sergeant from when Mark was about, and my new boss, Staff Hammond.

"I knew I recognised the name. This is the guy I told you about Rich," Zed told Staff Hammond as I introduced myself.

I knew it wouldn't be long before I was back in Dinger's spare room, so I had a chat with him to say, "Expect me".

The CO was a twat, just as Dinger had said. So with the re-formation came audits and re-inspections. This gave Zed and Staff Hammond about a million things to pick me up on. It took them about three weeks before they had me on RoP's for the inside of my beret being dirty.

Then, a few days later, the CO wanted a white-gloved room inspection, so Staff Hammond rubbed his fingers under my windowsill looking for dust. "And what do we have here, Baily?" Staff Hammond demanded, showing the CO his findings.

"A dirty glove Staff Sergeant; when was the last time you washed them?" the CO answered.

The fine dusting of chalk on his fingertips made the rest of his glove look grey in comparison. I had learnt some tricks while I was inside, so he didn't get it all his own way.

Soon my crewman Lee was moved into my room and dragged into the fold. He was asleep after a guard duty when I was on a re-inspection. Staff Hammond woke him up and we both had hourly locker inspections until well after midnight.

We fell out over it at first, but I organised his gear until the shouting came back to me. Then I begged, borrowed and bought a spare set of kit, packed and ready, for whichever one of us was on RoP's, so it became a game. Lee worried too much; I'd grown up like this, and spent too long in jail for them to beat me again.

I did get sent back to jail a few times, but that was like a holiday for me. In fact, I enjoyed my stays at Dinger's pleasure so much that I even sent myself there once.

I was on a guard patrol with a guy straight out of training, when his rifle goes off as he unloads it; then, he dropped it on the floor. I looked him up and down, shoved my rifle into his arms and picked his up. Then as I turned to the on-running Guard Commander I shouted, "It was me!" and got warned for Orders for a Negligent Discharge.

When I started my twenty-eight-day sentence, Dinger asked how I could be so stupid.

"That kid wouldn't have lasted ten minutes with you Staff...," I told him. "Still two sugars, is it?"

Along with Staff Hammond for comfort, I had the Regiment and the CO's exacting standards to meet as the BFT pass times are dropped by a minute. Not a problem for me, but there was a lot of people doing extra PT that didn't need to.

Then the CO went exercise barmy and was forever sending us out into the middle of nowhere for weeks on end. The day we arrived back at camp he'd decide we needed extra training, and had us doing forced marches through the night. Then we're straight back in the vehicles and off out for another few weeks of nowhere.

To get off camp and away from the regime, Lee and I volunteered for everything, which found us doing fatigues for the Nijmegen marches. The event itself is a hundred-mile walk over some of the bridges in Holland; we were going to be one of the water stops for the British soldiers taking part.

It was hard work setting up early each morning and then tearing down and moving on at night. But it was a carnival atmosphere all day and the weather was fantastic; and with beer guaranteed after we had finished work, we had a lot of fun.

Then we sloped off into town on the final day. At the club we went to, we both pulled a couple of Dutch hotties, and so became quite regular visitors for a while. (Sorry, this is the wrong type of book if you want those stories.)

Then there was a bit of a scare in Iraq over the search for weapons of mass destruction, so the CO blew it out of all proportion. He turned the focus of training to individual battle skills, and that suited Staff Hammond to a T.

Staff Hammond, like the CO, had served with the Commandos, so it became their goal that everyone should reach that level of battle readiness, and training became intense. Combat marches were now runs, with pass times being halved; exercises became weeks at a time in a field with nothing more than you could carry on your back, and the shouting never stopped.

The fatigue details changed too, so Lee and I were sent off to play enemy for someone. When we arrived, we were told some guys were going to be on the run and it was our job to catch them. There were a few basic survival skills we needed to learn first. So along with another dozen blokes, we joined in with the final few classes of the course.

A few days later, we were all bundled into the back of a truck, then dropped off a couple at a time at various points along the route, until it was mine and Lee's turn to get out.

"You're here and, I want you there. Don't get caught," this fat guy says, handing us a map and pointing out two places on it as he spoke. Then he got back in the truck and drove off.

The next morning, the same fat guy met us at the place we were told to be. He pointed to a new place on the map, and then we were off again. When we got to the new location, a bag was thrown over each of our heads and we were bundled into the back of a truck.

Sometime later we pulled up and were told to get out and sit back to back on the floor, still with our hoods on. I could hear Lee start to mutter his name, rank and number behind me. Then someone used us as a traffic cone to practise his hand brake turns around for a little while.

I got dragged off somewhere about half an hour later, only to be put into various painful stress positions to the sound of white noise. Personally, I was glad to be inside because it had started raining and I was getting cold. Later, I was laid out on a table and had a load of water poured over my head, still hooded, I didn't like that too much.

After the water torture treatment, I was taken into a room where some guy asked me far too loudly, what I'd seen over the last few days. I couldn't be bothered with another big shouty man by then, so I gave him the silent treatment until he threw me out.

"Enjoy your first taste of resistance to interrogation, did you sonny?" asked the fat guy who had dropped me off a few nights before.

"If that was supposed to make me talk, you need to have a word with my step mum mate. She never managed to get a word out of me either," I laughed, as I walked past him to get a brew.

When we got back to the Regiment, Lee was sent off parachuting and I found myself on a Weapons Handling course. I came back from that, and was straight off again to learn how to blow things up with the Pioneers. Then it was time to show Staff Hammond up again.

We were on a battle camp with him going on the whole time about the skinny runt he didn't want in his troop anymore. Then, on a patrol task in the middle of the night, one of the training staff orders us to walk up a path one at a time.

As the first guy sets off, there's a whoosh, bang, pop, when he sets off a booby trap, then he was brought back to the starting line. Lee cleared the course on his first attempt, and then it was my turn.

The first few traps were so obvious I ran past them without even pausing. With the next few, they were a little harder to see, so I thought I'd help out the others. I disabled the next half a dozen traps, and stowed the gear in my pockets until I reached the end.

When I finished, the training staff told me I had to put all the traps back where I'd found them, ready for Staff Hammond's attempt. He made it to within twenty feet of the finish line before all hell broke loose and every trap on the course triggered simultaneously.

I was close to tears as he warned me for Orders for wasting training resources. The training staff thought it was pretty funny though, and let me off.

The regiment changed again soon after that, and adventure training in Bavaria became the order of the day. That saw Lee and I being sent off to set up the admin areas and keep them clean while everyone had some fun.

Problem was, once everything was set up, there was nothing to do but have fun ourselves, so we started to go out with the local instructors. I had passed Grade 2 rock climbing and mountaineering before Staff Hammond and the rest of the troop arrived.

Still, I joined the troop for their fortnight of fun, and a

few days in I joined the mountain bikers for a day out. Up and down a few hills later, we end up having a liquid lunch on top of a big hill, and start thinking about the return journey.

Everyone wanted to head back as quickly as possible, so we decide to go straight down the side of the hill to the nearest road. We all set off, and after bouncing out of some woods, it opened up to a huge grass bank, so I started to relax back into the saddle, and looked down the hill for the road. But there was a hill going *up* in front of me. Before I knew it I was nearly forty feet in the air, having taken off from a ski jump!

This wasn't part of any plan. I was terrified!

After I stopped screaming I saw the ground rushing up towards me and tried to hold the landing together. I think I touched down okay, but then the front wheel seemed to collapse. So, head over heels, I landed in a heap at the bottom of the hill, with the wrecked bike next to me.

"Now that's what I joined the Army for!" I shouted back up at the ski jump.

Staff Hammond decided we were having too much fun with fatigues now, and started to bully poor Lee and me with constant guard duties. Lee got out of them first by joining the rugby team; he ended up playing semi-pro for a Dutch side. I didn't think such a rough sport was for me, so I went on guard.

Then the Regiment said they wanted volunteers for an inter-Squadron Boxing Match. And with both the CO and Staff Hammond never letting up, I decided I'd had enough time at home, and should go back to school for a bit. So I said, "I'll do it!"

I met the other lads who'd volunteered for the boxing team the following Monday for our pep talk. Coach went through how he had won the ABA Schoolboy Championship at fifteen, so, apparently he knew everything there was to know. Then it was off for a run.

For the next six weeks, every day would be the same. A run in the early morning before breakfast, then a mid-morning gym session; lunch would be followed by team sports, then into the boxing gym for a skills lesson, followed by dinner and knock-off. Within a fortnight we were all keeping pace with the extra physical training, and I started to really enjoy it. Then the card for fight night was drawn up.

"Super heavy, Johnson, you'll be fighting Wilkinson from Three Squadron," Coach announced. Johnson nodded before Coach went on.

"Heavyweight will be Tommy against Fisher...," He continued down the card, looking at each of us in turn.

"Bantamweight..., Dave, you've got a walkover," he said, eventually looking at me.

"What?" I shouted.

"You're the only Bantamweight in the Regiment, so you've already won mate. Congratulations." Coach said, holding out his hand as if I was to shake it.

"So I don't get to fight? Fuck that. I quit!" I screamed back, and walked out of the gym.

I changed my mind later when Coach said that I would put on a few pounds, and probably go up a weight class before fight night. And with that in mind, we looked at my diet.

That morning I had tipped the scales at 51.6 kg, the bottom end of my weight class. That meant I needed to gain 6 kg in less than four weeks. I was given a high protein diet at first, but within a few days my weight started to plummet. The only thing to do after that was to eat more.

Every day I had a double fry-up for breakfast, and steak for lunch. Dinner would nearly always be a Sunday-type roast and second puddings, with kebabs, pizza and cake for supper. A month later I weighed in at 51.5 kg. Any less would have seen me go down a weight class to Flyweight.

"I don't want to go out there tonight," I said to Coach as I got off the scales at the weigh-in.

"Think about the team Dave. Your walkover will give us a point head start; so come on, do it for them, if not yourself," he pleaded.

"I'm not going to do all that training to be laughed at for not fighting! I'm not going. Right!" I shouted back, and walked out the room.

A few minutes later, one of the guys in charge of the weigh-in joined me outside. He told me there was another lad in the Lightweight class who also had a walkover, so if I could get up to 56 kg, he would match us together. With only an hour before the weigh-in closed, I had no chance, so I walked off to the block.

Lee was ironing his kit in our room when I got back. I went to my locker and pulled out some uniform that I needed to iron myself, saying, "After you with that mate."

"Not fighting tonight?" he asked over his shoulder.

"Underweight. They want me to do a walkover, but I can't be bothered with the grief," I told him, dejected.

"You want to borrow some money?" Lee asked, putting the iron to one side.

"Nah, I've got a few bucks left, but cheers anyway." I said, after checking my wallet.

"Seriously, I've got loads." Lee threw me a bag of coins.

"Why didn't I think of that? Of course I want to borrow some money!" I smiled across, stuffing the bag in my pocket. An hour later, I tipped the scales at 57.1 kg, having decided to keep my tracksuit on this time.

"Now can I fight?" I asked the weigh-in panel.

"Lightweight. And yes Baily, you will be fighting tonight."

The rest of the day I psyched myself up for the job in

hand. I'd been told the guy's name, but it meant nothing to me. So without an opponent in my mind, I imagined meeting every bully I had ever come across in the ring that night.

Later in the gym, I was told mine was to be the first bout and got changed. After a quick warm-up with Coach, the first few bars of "Eye of the Tiger" played out, and I jogged slowly to the ring. I was so focused I didn't hear my name when I was introduced. Coach just raised my hand to an almighty cheer and took me to the centre of the ring.

"I want a good, clean fight...," the referee went on.

I wasn't listening; instead I just stared for the first time at the guy I'd be fighting. He was a good few inches taller than me, and looked like a brick outhouse. I wasn't bothered, he was just another guy who thought he could pick on me.

The bell sounded and we came back to the centre of the ring, each of us throwing a few light punches, looking for reactions. Then out of nowhere this right hand hit me like a sledgehammer, and the canvas appeared at eye level. I lay there for a moment, thinking a walkover hadn't been such a bad idea after all.

I got to my feet before the ref had finished his eight count, and he asked, "Where are we?"

"Are you stupid? We're in a boxing ring and you're the ref, or have you forgotten?" I smirked as I answered back.

"I'll have less of that..., Box!" he shouted, starting to step aside.

Before the ref raised his hand to let us at it again, a gloved fist hit me and the canvass came into view again. This time when I got up, the ref pointed me across to see the ringside doctor; then he went to warn the other bloke for his early punch. My nose was broken, but the doctor cleared me to continue. Not turning up definitely seemed a better idea now.

"Do you want to carry on?" the ref asked me when he came back over.

I nodded.

"Can you breathe?" he asked, staring into my eyes.

I blew a load of blood from my nose down my shirt. "Well enough!"

I was unsteady on my feet for the rest of the round, but I managed to throw a few decent punches, keeping me in the match, just. Then the ref came to my corner during the interval, warning that he would stop the fight if I didn't defend myself better.

Round two started with this guy running across the ring to finish me off. I took a side step and he ran straight into the corner post. Changing my balance slightly, I threw a punch in his direction, hitting him between the eyes as he turned around.

He took a standing eight count, and we became even on the nose front, but he came back well. Then towards the end of the round, I felt his demon right hook again. Though I didn't go down, I still took another eight count.

Coach still reckoned us about even on points as we touched gloves for the start of the third and final round. Then the first minute of it was just a barrage of punches going both ways, before I got yet another standing count.

The punch that caught me didn't hurt, and as I came back to centre ring I saw this guy's shoulder drop, ready to throw his demon right. This time I'd seen it early enough to send an uppercut his way, hitting him squarely on the jaw.

His eyes rolled to the back of his head as his legs turned to jelly, and he went down like a rag doll. Then the bell sounded the end of the match before the ref started his count.

Back in my corner, Coach tried to convince me that I had a chance of taking the match. A few minutes later, after the judges had totted up their scorecards, we were called back to centre ring to hear the result. As the announcement started, I knew I had three standing counts against his two, but was proud that I'd gone the distance either way.

"My lords, ladies and gentlemen, we have a split decision, with all three judges scoring the bout a dead heat, but we do have a winner." came over the PA system, "So, by the referee's decision, I give to you the winner of the first Lightweight bout of the evening – Private Dave Baily!"

I looked at the ref as he raised my hand in the air, and then the chants from the crowd came in unison. "Baily! – Baily! – Baily! –"

The chanting got louder as I ran to the ropes and screamed my victory at Staff Hammond and the officers. Then I ran to each side of the ring, my screams of victory, answered by my name over and over again.

After the glory of the ring, the changing rooms were a sombre affair. Mine was the first of fifteen bouts that night, so congratulations went many ways in the bar later. But before that came the award ceremony, and each boxer was given his winner's or runner's-up trophy. My squadron also won the team trophy, and as it was announced I was pushed forward to receive it, to yet more cheering.

Then I was amazed to hear my name called yet again as I was given the Golden Glove award for best boxer of the night. I was high for a week with the buzz of it all.

A few days after the fight, I was told to report to Major Jackson. I didn't know the name, and so, after getting a few directions to his office, I was surprised to see the referee from the fight behind the desk.

"The next time a referee asks you a question, don't give him a snarky answer. You got that?" the Major said after I introduced myself.

"Sorry sir. I won't," I replied, guilty as charged.

"Right, bollocking over," he continued. "I'm putting

together a Regimental team, and you're in it. Report to the gym next Monday at six. You're on leave till then. Now, who's your troop Staffy so I can give him the good news?"

I kept my winning streak going for my next three fights, and then I lost to a guy from Three Para. It only took him forty-five seconds to knock me out, then I was taken to his corner to recover.

When I heard the bell ring, sounding the fight was over; I raced out of the corner thinking it was the start of the second round. Thankfully, someone grabbed me before I hit anyone: that might have got me a six-month ban from the ring.

My record was pretty good, and for the next twelve months or so, I built it to eight wins out of ten, four of them by knockout. Then talk started about me being awarded my Army Colours for Boxing Achievements and joining the Army boxing team. I even heard the '96-Olympics and my name mentioned in the same sentence more than once.

I picked up an injury to my shoulder around that time during a training session. I had to have a minor operation to one of the tendons so I couldn't do any physical training for four weeks.

Reporting back to my troop and Staff Hammond with a light duties chit. He put me on guard duty – day on, day off – for the two weeks I would actually spend in the troop after my sick leave; so I could make up for the ones I'd missed while I was boxing.

Major Jackson didn't like that, and got me posted out of the squadron within three days of me coming back from leave. I still stayed on the same camp, but would be working for the REME in the Generator Repair Bay until I could start training again. Then I was going to be moved to the gym full time.

I'd been with my new troop for about two weeks when

they all went off for a regular sports afternoon. I was still banned from training at the time, so with some important work still needing to be done that day, I offered to finish it up. Later, as the lads came back, I was just doing the final touches when someone brought the forklift truck into the workshop for the night.

"MOVE!" someone screamed.

I turned in the direction of the voice and was hit in the back; then the forklift veered past with no one driving. It had hit me in the pelvis and pushed my knee into the generator I was working on, snapping my femur in two.

I laid back and died.

In fact, I died twice, but the paramedics were pretty good at their jobs. Then I remember waking up in the operating theatre, but that was such a surreal experience it's hard to put into words. Anyway, the following morning I pulled the sheet back to see my leg in traction.

The next week became one long medical test after another. Then the surgeon asked me one day when I'd last been in a car crash. I told him never, as he pointed out twenty-seven damaged bones on a full body x-ray that they'd taken when I was admitted. I explained that I'd been bullied once or twice, he seemed happy enough with that.

His main concern, of course, was my femur, for which he put a full-length pin into, along with some staples in my pelvis for a hair line fracture. The operation went okay, but it was a few months before I was fit again, by then priorities had changed.

Chapter 16
Life Without . . . Benny

Preparations for Bosnia were well underway when I came back from sick leave. It was no surprise; for weeks, there had been nothing on the news other than the ethnic cleansing and the mass graves being discovered over there.

On camp, the boxing had been shelved and everyone was focused on getting vehicles and equipment ready, pending a full Regimental deployment. A month later, I was on guard duty and waved almost every member of the Regiment off to war. I wouldn't be going anywhere until I was off the sick.

Staying on camp during the deployment meant I would have the monotonous routine of Duty Driver for the Guard, or litter picking. Sometimes, if I was lucky, I might get to re-paint some kerbstones, one of the usual tasks I'd have to do if I found myself in jail.

The boredom of it all, and not being allowed to do any physical training, soon saw me diagnosed with depression. The doctor on camp prescribed me some anti-depressants, but if you asked me, I'd say they didn't really help.

A few weeks later, it was no surprise to find me reporting to the guardroom as Duty Driver. There were that few of us left on camp, we were all pulling a duty every three days or so. Then, during the morning briefing, I was told that I'd need to pick up some guy, Charlie, from his house to take him to a nearby camp to catch a lift back to the UK.

At about one the following morning, I was knocking on his door as expected, and after putting his bags in the Rover we set off. The camp I was heading for wasn't too far away, and during the drive Charlie told me that he was going back home for a cricket tournament he was playing in that weekend.

We arrived in what should have been plenty of time for him to get his next lift, but after checking the accommodation block, and then the signing-out book at their guardroom, we discovered that they had left about half an hour before we got there. Charlie tried to blame me for picking him up late; and though it wasn't my fault, I said that I'd try to help him out, by racing his mates to the border with Holland.

We set off, and as soon as I got on the Autobahn my foot went to the floor, taking the V8 Rover to well over a hundred mph. About forty minutes later, I pulled into the last service station before the border. Here, just about every squaddie who drove back to the UK would stop and fill their car, using fuel tokens they'd brought cheap back on camp. Most would also change their money or take some form of break before the long drive to Calais, again the normal squaddie ferry crossing, so I was expecting to find Charlie's mates there.

I dropped him off at the doors to the services, so he could search for them inside, while I checked outside for their car. A few minutes later, we met back up, neither of us having any luck.

Once Charlie was back in the Rover, I set off again at a more sedate pace, intending to turn round at the next exit, but all the while I was driving he was telling me to speed up, because, he thought we couldn't be more than ten minutes behind his mates. That didn't matter to me because in less than five minutes we would be at the border crossing, though I did try to keep him happy by going to the last exit I could.

I was driving a military vehicle, in uniform, armed with a 9 mm pistol, and didn't have my passport or any papers with me, so there was no way I was going to get through the main border crossing as it came into sight.

Charlie had other ideas, and kept on and on that we

should go through. I pulled over on the hard shoulder to try to explain that we would have to turn back, but then he revealed his rank of Staff Sergeant and ordered me to keep going.

I gave in to his order, but still turned off the Autobahn for a lesser-used crossing, hoping they would just turn me around rather than call the RMPs. I didn't know it at the time, but this crossing was often unmanned, and soon I was on the Dutch Autobahn, chasing down the elusive car.

Holland isn't a very big country, so, with the detour and the stops we'd made, I had little to no chance of catching Charlie's mates before the border with Belgium. It didn't stop him ordering me to cross that one too. I just held up my hand to shut him up when the French border came into view.

We arrived in Calais at around seven that morning without getting stopped, and about three hours before Charlie's ferry was due to board, so I parked as far away from the terminal building as I could.

As a gesture of his thanks Charlie then offered to buy me breakfast, so, I borrowed a tracksuit from him and tried to hide the fact that I had a pistol hidden under it. After we had eaten, I sat in the waiting area to take a nap before my drive back.

Charlie nudged me back to my senses about an hour later and introduced his mates. They'd only just arrived, explaining that they had been at McDonald's when I arrived to drop Charlie off. I didn't find it as funny as they did, and stormed off.

Luck was on my side again, and I managed to avoid getting stopped at the border crossings on the way back. So arriving back at camp late that afternoon, I reported to the guardroom to hand over my duty, about ten hours later than I should have.

"Where the fuck have you been Baily?" the Guard commander shouted as I handed my pistol back in.

"That twat last night ordered me to take him to the ferry, so where the fuck do you think I've been?" I shouted back.

"What? You took him to Calais?" he asked in disbelief.

I nodded in reply.

"You stupid bastard. Get in there!" he screamed, pointing to the cells.

After I had written my statement, no one could work out what to charge me with. An armed soldier on duty, crossing just one border without permission, isn't just breaking military and civil law; it breaches the Geneva Convention. So effectively I had just committed an act of war and single-handedly invaded half of Europe! They decided on Treason in the end, with a warning that I could still face a firing squad for that.

I knew execution was unlikely but, I was still crapping myself because, instead I would be looking at life in prison if found guilty. Then thankfully for me, Charlie owned up to ordering me through at the border crossings when he got back.

I'm not sure what he got charged with, but he was bust down to Private and had to serve three years in jail before his discharge. My stupidity was blamed on the anti-depressants; that got my driving privileges removed by the doctor, leaving me just the rubbish and kerbstones to deal with.

Weeks of boredom went by until, one morning I was tasked to clean a vehicle that had just come back from Bosnia. They said it had been involved in some kind of accident, and when I saw three neat holes in the roof, and blood everywhere, what kind of accident became clear.

I had a strong stomach and, even as my eyes rolled to the back of my head from the anti-depressants, I knew the job had to be done by someone. I won't go into the details of it, but over the next few hours I improved the look of the cab.

Then, once I'd found the vehicle documents, I checked some details, and an envelope fell from the folder they were in. The neatly folded sheet of paper inside was a letter containing this man's final words, written in his own fair hand.

"I'll see his family gets this Baily," the workshop Sergeant said as I handed him the letter.

"Benny was my roommate, Sarg," I whispered, and lost the plot.

I was sent on compassionate leave, but that was just a haze of drink and drug abuse. I suppose the next clear memory I have was being brought back to camp in handcuffs a month later.

Then as I was jailed for going AWOL, the icing on the cake came. Declared unfit for detention, I ended up in hospital having psychological evaluations. Re-diagnosed with Post Traumatic Stress Disorder that brought on my childhood memories, I was sent back to camp two weeks later.

While in hospital I was weaned off the drugs and cleared to start physical training. And soon the psychiatrist, who I was still seeing daily, thought the best thing for me would be to join my friends out in Bosnia. After that, I spent most of my free time concentrating on strengthening my leg and getting back to full fitness.

I landed in a Croatian airport about six weeks later. A few days passed and I was off again to Sarajevo with half a dozen other lads. Then, on our final approach to the airport, gunfire started and our helicopter dropped out of the sky.

"Sorry about that lads, but we're soft-skinned. Did anyone get hurt back there?" the pilot asked over the intercom. Everybody was okay – but what a wake-up call!

There was shooting going on most nights throughout the early months I was in Bosnia. But generally, during daylight hours, work for us would go on as normal. For my part, that meant being a mobile engineer sorting out various broken-down generators around the country. Manpower was tight and many of these trips I would undertake alone. However, the routes I'd use were regularly patrolled, so help, if needed, was never far away.

I'd been in Bosnia about three weeks when I was sent to a compound in the centre of the country. The French ran it, although as with most compounds, a British signals troop was handling our own communications.

I had been working on my own towards the back of the compound for a few hours, when all hell broke loose somewhere near the entrance. Everyone inside the walled-off area started shouting and ran to the defence perimeter. Then the British commander pointed me towards a space at the wall, and told me where I was to cover, along with my orders for opening fire.

I never found out what started it, but whatever happened at the gate was over quickly, and was replaced by a screaming crowd. As the minutes passed, the crowd grew, eventually splitting into smaller groups dotted around the compound.

The area me and the other Brits were covering was pretty quiet, with just one small group who were more like onlookers than part of any kind of protest. Then, as I'm scanning the area, I see a bloke sitting on the ground on his own.

A few minutes passed and he stood up, took a few steps, and sat back down again. Another few minutes pass and he moved again.

He was a good distance from anyone else, so I called for the Brit Commander, wanting to tell him we might have someone laying mines. As I shout, this guy stands up, and turning around I see the rifle in his hands.

As he starts to fire off his machine gun on full automatic; I cocked and pulled the trigger on my own rifle, hitting him in the shoulder, I think, making him stumble and fall backwards. I was right about the mines: he fell on one.

Everyone in our area ran off and wouldn't come back, so nothing else happened near us, though a few shots were fired from elsewhere around the compound. About an hour later everything was over and the clean-up operation started. I had no involvement with that so, after writing out a contact report, I was on my way back to Sarajevo a few hours later.

Coming under fire was a rarity but accidents on the other hand were rife. Most of the bridges were blown up during the conflict, so unstable tracks around the mountainside where used as roads. But if you veered off the hard surface, you would most likely be in the middle of a minefield.

One morning about five months into my tour, I was told to follow the Recovery Mechanic and help him on a job. When we arrived at the accident we saw two trucks with a bloke trapped between them.

The medics were already there keeping the guy stable. But as I helped the Recovery Mechanic we both knew what would happen when we pulled the vehicles apart. Then just as I put the last strap in place, the trapped guy called me to him.

"Tell my wife that I love her…," He did say a lot more, but when I wrote it down, I added the last few lines he didn't have time for.

His wife called to ask if I would talk at his funeral back in the UK. I politely declined, blaming it on another operation I was due to have. In reality, I didn't want his family asking about his last few minutes. He seemed like a decent bloke and should be remembered for his life, not the way he lost it.

I didn't actually know about the operation until I started my R & R leave. It was timed so that I could have a routine check-up on my leg. When the x-ray came back it showed that the 18-inch nail, which should have been holding my leg together, had moved. The following morning they took it out.

The bone had healed by then and I was back on my feet within a few days and sent on sick leave. Then over the coming weeks I kept up with my physiotherapy, so I was soon cleared to return to Bosnia.

Bosnia is a beautiful country so, I was looking forward to my first trip out, a few days after arriving back. As with most of my trips off base, that day started with a drive down the aptly nicknamed Sniper Alley. I'd driven the route hundreds of times before and, there hadn't been an incident in the area for months, so I wasn't worried about it, but today a single shot rang out.

I could tell the shot had been close but I didn't find out how close until I limped my vehicle into a nearby friendly base. The round had gone through the front wing of the Rover I was driving and cracked the engine block.

What you hear in the movies about a rifle having a distinctive sound when it's fired, especially when it's fired at you, is completely true. So in my contact report, I gave details of distance, direction, and even the fact that I thought the shooter had used a Dragunov, a common sniper rifle around at that time.

A few days passed with not a lot going on, and then a couple of SAS guys came into my workshop on base. "You the lad that got shot at?" one of them asked.

I nodded.

"I've been up to see your mate and told him to stop shooting at people, he won't bother you again matey," he said calmly. "And thanks for letting us know about the rifle; probably wouldn't have bothered looking for it if you hadn't said." He added before they walked off.

Make no mistake: I know exactly how the SAS tell people to stop shooting. An image of this man's shocked face as his door was blown off its hinges filled my mind. That was replaced by the image of his grieving family over his bullet-ridden body, wanting vengeance on the murderous bastard responsible. I may not have pulled the trigger, but I was responsible for that man's death.

The feeling of guilt grew as my past came back to haunt me; soon I was blaming myself for every death I heard about, whether I knew them or not. And without work to take my mind off things, my nights became full of self-pity and guilt. I made the decision that I wasn't going to leave Bosnia.

Finding a gun was easy enough: I slept with mine every night I was out there, literally. With the *how* sorted, I set about telling myself the reasons *why*. When I'd finished, I packed a few hundred sheets of paper into a folder.

"Take this for 'us mate." I asked the guy I was sharing a room with, passing him the folder.

"What do you want me to do with it?" he replied, taking it from me.

"Don't really care to tell you the truth. Chuck it if you want, I'm getting out of here soon anyway," I told him, and left for work. Today was the day.

I'd been given a detail way up in the mountains, and wouldn't be expected back for a few days. As I drove to the location I'd been given, I steered off route and up one of the passes. There I found somewhere to stop, parking the Rover on the edge of a cliff.

Sitting on the bonnet, I thought about what I was about to do. I reckoned that if I did this right, my body would fall in the ravine and never be found; I'd be classed as Missing in Action: a hero's death, for those who cared for me.

My mind was completely calm when I took my pistol out of its holster and readied it for action. I thought of the folder I'd given my roommate telling him of my Life Without…, and relaxed.

Someone will know, ran through my mind. *He'll read about Life Without Mum, and he'll know what Life Without the Frost's turned into. He'll understand what Life Without Mark did to me, and why Life Without Clare hurts so much. And he'll know why now it's time for me to join her.*

"Clare's not here and you know it!" Mark's voice shouted from somewhere deep within my head. *"Now think! Think about leave! Think!"*

A barrage of random thoughts replaced the calmness until, through a smoky haze, I saw Clare. She was twelve; I was putting a necklace around her neck that I'd bought for her birthday. It was the last time I saw her before I was taken away as a kid.

Then the image changed and I saw her as an adult; she was scowling at me like I had something on my shoe. There were kids too. Her kids? I remembered playing with them on the floor in front of her. And later that night, was it her baby that slept on my lap?

It didn't make sense. I'd been told Clare had died just after I joined the Army; I'd never seen her as an adult, so she couldn't have had kids, she was too young the last time we met. Then the haze started to clear.

I was on leave; drugged up to the eyeballs on anti-depressants, and so drunk I could hardly stand. Compassionate leave, eight short months ago, just after Benny died. That could only mean one thing: Clare was still alive!

It wasn't much, but it was a start. I put my pistol back in its holster and cried for a few hours. The bad things in my life were still there, of course, but so were the good things. All I'd achieved just by joining the Army, how I'd recovered after Mark's death, then the rock climbing and boxing. I wanted to tell Clare everything and make her proud of me. I couldn't do that if I was dead, could I.

With that thought, I cleaned myself up, checked the map, and got back on route. Then, as I rounded a corner half an hour later, I saw five large discs blocking the road. Each one had a rod sticking up from it: anti-tank mines!

As I stopped, two guys blocked my rear with more mines, and three more guys appeared from the bushes to the front of me. It wasn't uncommon to see this type of thing when you were crossing a border, but I was in the middle of nowhere. Still, I acted as I should have and got out of the Rover, leaving my rifle behind so as not to look threatening.

Looking for the commander's rank badge, I then offered him a sheet of paper identifying who I was, and why I was in the area, written in the local dialects.

He shouted something and one of his men levelled a rifle at me.

Before I knew it, I'd drawn my pistol and fired a round past the commander's ear. "If I couldn't do myself, then you'll die before me!" I screamed.

"Okay, okay," the commander shouted back, batting down his man's weapons. "We move, you go. No trouble, okay? ..., See? You go now okay." Then he moved one of the mines to the side of the track himself.

I kept my pistol trained on him until I was clear of the line of mines, then gunned the Rover to get out of firing range quick. Adrenalin was still well and truly kicked in ten minutes later, when I saw another guy in uniform. At least this time I recognised it as a British Army pattern.

"I'm Jimmy, what's your name sonny?" he asked, opening the passenger door and climbing into the Rover.

"Baily, Dave Baily." I said, before asking "Echo-Bravo?" – A code question.

"We don't bother with that crap up here, now do you see the third tree from the left? Stop there, we've got a couple of lads that would like a lift up the hill," he said, pointing up the track.

There were three lads waiting near the tree as I pulled up. They came over and chatted to Jimmy for a moment, before asking me about the gunshot they'd heard. I told them briefly what had happened, and the three of them jogged down the road to "have a word" with the Serbians, while I took Jimmy back to the campsite.

We settled down for the evening and soon a raging fire was on the go. When the other lads came back, we introduced ourselves properly, and started to chat as if we were old mates. Then the subject of the roadblock came up.

Now I have eaten with Royalty and had the famous call me their friend. I've climbed the Zugspitze, where I stood on top of the world, and I once had over four thousand people screaming my name after winning a championship-boxing match.

But gaining the respect of those four SAS guys, as I retold my story in more detail; passing a bottle of local hooch around a campfire, on a mountaintop in the middle of nowhere. That was by far the greatest feeling of my life. And for a moment, I felt like a god.

The next morning, Jimmy woke me up and everyone got ready for the day ahead. There wasn't really anything I had to do except drop off some spare parts, so after breakfast, along with Jimmy, we set off to another campsite.

We talked a lot along the way about Bosnia and what was going on. The main hostilities with the Serbs and Croats had calmed by then, so the British forces had started to help rebuild the country.

I played my part in what's called the Hearts and Minds campaign, by helping to rewire a building so it could be used as a school. And when the mains electricity was turned back on, I helped out again, taking some of the generators off line. Jimmy and the rest of the SAS were playing their part too, training up the local police forces so they could look after themselves when we eventually pulled out of the country.

On the way back to our campsite that evening, Jimmy pointed off in the direction of a mass grave that had been uncovered a few months before. I've been sent to one myself, and I can tell you they're not a pretty sight; but that wasn't what was playing on my mind.

"How do you cope?" I asked, after he'd finished his tale.

"It's just part of the job we've got sonny, so you have to try and switch off." Jimmy replied.

"I can't: every time I close my eyes I can see his face, and the fear in his eyes, knowing he's only got seconds left to live." I whispered back.

"What'd you do?" He asked. Speaking quietly I told Jimmy about the guy I shot.

Jimmy thought for a few moments before saying, "Sounds to me like you did the right thing. Just think, it might have been you going home in a body bag, and I'm sure your folks back home wouldn't want that."

"Ha! Don't get me started about my folks," I laughed, "But I know: better him than me, or some kid just out playing. It's just watching it happen. I can't get it out of my mind."

"Yeah, I know what you mean. Suppose for me it's the training: it kind of prepares you for it, but; can I ask you something?" Jimmy said, looking across at me.

"Go for it!" I replied.

"At the ridge, why didn't you jump?" Jimmy asked. I looked back at him as though I didn't know what he was talking about before he went on, "We're an observation post up here. You were there far too long to be checking a map and; well it's obvious to me now that you weren't lost in the first place – so, go on."

"Thought of a girl I met back home, she always knew

how to cheer me up," I chuckled as I started to remember that drunken night at Clare's a bit clearer.

"Ahh, young love, works every time," Jimmy said with a smile, and relaxed back into his seat.

"Nar, it's not like that, in fact I thought she'd died years ago, so just to see her so alive, so happy, it was just amazing." I told him, then tried to gesture how intense the feeling was, my words unequal to it.

"So you going to see her again?" he asked.

"Don't know, maybe. She's married now with kids so she'll probably think I'm only trying it on. Just knowing she's happy will do for now, especially while I'm out here anyway." I told him, the news of it all still a bit of a shock to my system.

"Maybe you should go and see her. Think she'd like to know a brave guy like you – I know I'm glad that I got to meet you sonny," he said, patting me on the shoulder.

"One day, maybe." I smiled back, and got on to happier subjects, telling him how I'd once attempted to take over Europe.

I wish I could have stayed there longer, but the following morning Jimmy said we had one drop to make, and then he needed a lift back to Sarajevo. I think he wanted to make sure I got back all right, but I was glad of the company.

Chapter 17

My roommate had left on R & R by the time I got back to base, so I didn't really think about the folder I'd given him. Then one day, I joined the other lads in the workshop tearoom for a break and, someone turned on the radio as usual.

"We've a special 'Our Tune' here that we're going to air over the next few days," said the DJ through the speaker. "It's a heart-warming story from one of the lads out there with you today. It's a little longer than we would normally like, but here we go with someone's *Life Without....*"

I stopped what I was doing and listened in amazement. "My name is Danny Brady and I was born in Bedfordshire towards the end of 1970, then from what I've been told I was taken to Yorkshire soon after," the DJ continued.

I went out for a smoke while everyone else listened to Danny's remarkably similar story to my own, of his struggle through a violent childhood. Then, for the next four days, the war seemed to stop for an hour each day as his story continued, until one day Danny joined the Army, becoming a champion boxer, and each day's reading ending with 'Eye of the Tiger'.

"You been listening to Our Tune Dave?" asked Jodie, one of the girls I worked with, seeing me standing alone in the smoking area.

"Nar, same old drivel about someone's wife has run off with the cat, or the guy's son wants to marry the family dog. Getting bored of 'em," I replied.

She chuckled, "You should have heard this one mate. It's been going on for days now about this bloke's whole life, and some of the things this guy's Dad did were horrid, but he wouldn't leave his sister with him, even after he found out he wasn't his real Dad."

"Tough kid, I take it he was okay in the end?" I asked, playing dumb.

"That's the thing you see, he joined the Army when he was old enough, and, he's out here somewhere. Just goes to show what a true survivor he is." Jodie said, showing her admiration.

"Looks like he's got a secret admirer here." I laughed.

"As if, but wouldn't any girl like a big brother like…," Jodie trailed off and stared at me for a moment. "He's you."

I nodded.

"Oh – my – god! How did you cope?" she gasped.

"Don't know. Suppose it was just normal life for me," I said, shrugging my shoulders.

"I don't know how anyone could treat you like that. Do you still talk to your family?" Jodie asked.

"Sometimes, you know, forgive and forget type thing, but to tell you the truth this is where my family is now." I held up my hands and spun full circle, to gesture that I meant every soldier around me.

"Aww, that's sweet. Have you ever thought about writing a book?" Jodie suggested, taking my hand and giving it a reassuring squeeze.

"Need a happy ending first…, fancy getting married?" I proposed with a cheeky grin.

"Well, that's an offer most girls would jump at. But I think my boyfriend might have something to say about it." She let out a laugh before asking. "Really, what are you going to do?"

"I don't know, maybe I'll have a go at joining the SAS next," I replied. "What do you reckon?"

She put her hand on one side of my face and gently kissed the other side. "You'll make it, I know you will."

We carried on chatting for a few minutes before we went back to work, though, I asked Jodie not to tell anyone that I was Danny.

Over the next few days I re-joined the lads in the tearoom for break, listening to the same old drivel again. But after the drivel now, everybody would end up talking about Danny and his life. I would never add anything to the discussions, though listening to people talk about my life, with such respect and admiration for what I'd achieved. That lifted me in a way I couldn't believe.

I didn't think seriously about joining the SAS until I met Jimmy again a few weeks later. When I told him what I'd said to Jodie, I was expecting him to laugh his head off but instead he advised,

"Guys like you, who can get up and carry on, tend to do well in The Regiment. Selection will be extra tough for you, so you'll have to show your worth first. Start by passing as many courses as you can, then the training staff might give you a bit of leeway, if you're very lucky."

We carried on talking about my military experience so far and Jimmy seemed to think that I already had a lot in my favour. He went on to suggest a few courses I should try, adding that I needed to be outstanding in all of them, before I stood any chance of having my application passed. He then went on with more advice about the selection course itself, telling me a couple of pit falls that had caught him out.

Passing courses is one thing, but getting into any Special Forces unit is another thing altogether, and the British SAS Selection course is regarded as the toughest in the world. The endurance phase was what worried me.

Each day you're sent out on a forced march, with the distance and the weight you carry going up each time. A few weeks later and it's onto test week, finishing with the 'Long Drag', and a forty-mile march across the Welsh mountains in less than twenty hours.

Sound easy? Well, remember the mountains? You'll

be walking a lot further than forty miles, I can tell you. How far depends on your map-reading skills. And by the way, you'll also be carrying 55 lb. on your back, plus the weight of your water, rations and rifle for the day.

Still sound easy? At the time I weighed 51.5 kg (113 lb.), fighting weight. My fitness level was good, but maybe not that good. But even with this immense physical challenge ahead, Jimmy made it all seem so achievable. So when I said my goodbyes' to him later I had started to wonder if I could.

I still had a few months of my tour in Bosnia left to go, but I started to up my physical training using the well-equipped gym on the base. Most of the guys assumed that I had started to think about boxing again, and, that was fine by me. For now I just wanted to test how far I could push myself.

Training in the gym was fine but I also needed to train with my Bergen on my back. At the time we had a lull in our workload so, I asked my boss about joining some of the patrols still going on.

After giving me a queer look, he said okay and I soon found myself walking around the city every few days. The patrols weren't anything to write home about, just hours of walking in circles really; but it was nice to see people slowly getting back to a normal way of life.

Then the week before I was due to fly out of Bosnia for the last time, my boss called me to the command vehicle with news of my new posting. I was to go back to Germany and pack, then when my R & R finished report to my new unit back in the UK.

"You happy with that Baily?" my OC asked.

One posting is much the same as any other to me, though I had noticed that I would be attached to the REME again. That was a bonus for me so I smiled and nodded.

"Once you get there have a word with China. He'll have some good advice for you if you're serious about this, and, good luck Danny." He said as we shook hands. I don't know if Jodie told him, but, now my confidence had reached boiling point.

China was my new boss and I met him about six weeks later. After I introduced myself it became clear that my old OC had been speaking to him. Early in our conversation he brought up the subject of my training, giving me a few routes to build my endurance, while carrying a Bergan. When I was given the chance, I asked about going on a Temperate Survival course that I'd heard about.

"Impress me first, then I'll let you have some fun." China offered.

He joined me the first few times I went tabbing so it didn't take long for me to impress, then courses came thick and fast. First came a few days map reading, and to keep in practice I joined the orienteering team. First Aid and Field Craft Techniques followed soon after, then came a Detachment Commanders' course.

I had to do well on this one and got off to a good start, scoring highly in my physical assessment, and again with my lesson about how a generator works. Then during the third week I got to show off again with first aid.

During the final test week of the course we were sent out into the woods as a fighting troop. As the week progressed various scenarios were set up so we each got a chance to command a patrol. When it came to my turn to take control, I was to lead a four-man team.

The scenario was that we were in hostile territory with an enemy force in the area. My team and I had to navigate, at night, to a place about eight miles away, where we should find a rations cache. If we came across any enemy on route we should also gather as much intelligence as we could without breaking cover. Then the instructor would assess my leadership and everyone's military skills.

I briefed the lads in more detail than I needed to, because that was what was expected on the course, and we set off, joined by the instructor.

I'd chosen quite a long route out, hoping to avoid contact with the enemy until we had the cache, but we still arrived in the right area in good time. Then I left my team in a ditch so I could scope out the area myself before I placed my lookouts.

The rations should have been buried just inside a wooded area across the track in front of me, according to the information I was given, but I could see the two boxes in open sight. Ten metres further up the track there was a Rover parked in some bushes, with two guys playing enemy sitting on the bonnet.

They were talking about how they're going to win a crate of beer if we fail to get the rations, and how they'll wait till well after sun up if they needed too. The instructor had joined me part-way through their conversation, so he knew what was going on before I went back to the team I was leading.

"We've been set up lads. These guys have found the cache and are guarding it," I updated them, out of earshot of the enemy. "So our options are, we turn back now and fail the task," I paused before stating option two, "–we wait it out and hope we've got enough time to get back."

"Sounds like you've got a third option," the instructor suggested.

I smiled before saying, "Or we go back with prisoners."

The rest of my team smiled back, nodding, but the instructor didn't want us to get too physical in the capture, saying, "No prisoners." So I quickly came up with a new plan of swinging around to approach the Rover from behind. There we split into two fire-teams and take them out from a safe distance with rifles –

blank rounds, of course.

The bushes that the Rover was parked in were so thick that we could get right on top of the enemy without being seen. So from near point-blank range, the four of us emptied our magazines from just behind these two guys.

The noise of a hundred and twenty blank rounds being fired off on full automatic was ear-shattering in the still night air, but we were expecting it. Those guys didn't know what hit them.

One froze solid, as if caught in the headlights of a truck, holding on to the bonnet of the Rover for dear life and wet himself. The other set off down the track screaming for his mother to come and help him, and had to be brought back by the instructor a few moments later. It was absolutely hilarious to watch, but, we were all hyped up so stayed in character for the scenario.

"Bodies in the Rover! Pick me up over there!" I screamed at the lads as I broke cover and made for the rations, which I threw in the back as the lads arrived with our passengers on board.

I hadn't really planned for this part, so, with a quick bit of map-reading I chose a place to dump the Rover a few miles away. Then as we drove, the rations were split into the empty packs we'd brought for the job, and our bodies were relieved of their maps and cigarettes.

They weren't best pleased at that, and started to come back to life, so I thought we'd be better off tying up zombies with their bootlaces, before they infected the locals. Then, abandoning the Rover and zombies in some woods a little later, we ran off into the night with the keys.

Still a few miles from our campsite, I planned another route, again using the cover of the land hoping not to meet any more enemy. Though it was a bit harder going than I expected, we arrived back just before dawn. Being the last team in, everyone else was sat in the centre of camp, getting bollocked about the night's events.

"And what's your excuse, Baily?" the course IC asked as I came into view.

"Staff? What for Staff?" I said, taking what was now quite a heavy pack off my back.

"Getting into contact like these Muppets and coming back, no doubt, empty-handed," he shouted back.

By the time he'd finished there was enough food for twenty men at my feet. "Dumped a couple of zombies about four miles away, so they won't be bothering us for a while. Oh, by the way, I know where their camp is too," I said, and fished into my pocket for the enemy's map.

The course IC started clapping, and was soon joined by everyone else. Most of the other teams would say they had been set up too, of course. But having either been ambushed on route to their cache, or got lost, no one else had come back with their supplies, let alone any intelligence.

In my debriefing a little later I wasn't faulted on a single thing, although they never give out a perfect score. That also meant that I'd proved my worth as a commander, and so, for the rest of the course, other people made the plans, and I was content just to follow them.

Between courses my endurance training became relentless. Each day after work I would put on my Bergan for a ten-mile run, and over the weekends I'd be found going over the Yorkshire Dales for mile upon mile. After about nine months of this I was fitter and stronger than I've ever been before, so I asked China if he thought I was ready.

"Read that," he said, passing me a Forces magazine.

As I read the article, he filled in the details of a fun run, 70 kilometres (43 miles) around the Bavarian foothills. Army teams were entering as part of a competition, with a target time of twenty-four hours.

"I can have a word with a mate of mine and get you into a team that's been training for it. They'll only be carrying about 25 lb. but, if you keep up with them, I'll pass your application. Deal?" China offered.

"Can I do it as an individual rather than in the squad?" I asked. He said he'd check and we shook on the deal.

I arrived in Bavaria about three weeks later with half a dozen other lads. There was no problem with me going it alone on the march, so as we booked in, I was given a different start time and directions to the camping area. At around four the next morning I was woken up.

After a hearty breakfast, I made my way to the start holding area and checked over the map. It was a simple eleven-mile course around one of the lower peaks, fairly flat overall, and you couldn't get lost unless you really tried to. Then, at oh-four-fifty, someone said, "Go!" and off I went.

China said I should try to finish the march still carrying 30 lb., but even with the added weight of my rations it sat well on my back. I had trained with this kind of weight before, but, this was by far the longest single tab I'd attempted, so I knew I had to pace myself. Still within an hour or so there's no one in sight and I'm wondering why I didn't bring my Walkman.

Then I rounded a bend and a mountain gale hit me in the face like an avalanche. My back was soaked in sweat from carrying my Bergan so the icy wind chilled me to the bone. After an hour of this torment, seeming to make no headway, I sat behind a rock thinking about throwing in the towel.

"Do you think I want a man that quits as easily as you?" Clare's voice said from somewhere in my mind. My whole body hurt with the cold, but with a smile I stood up and dusted myself off.

"Guess not." I said aloud and set off again.

I hadn't tried to get in touch with Clare since I realised she was alive. In all fairness, I'd hardly even thought about her until then; but with nothing else to take my mind off the pain, I chatted to her for a while – or, should I say, to myself. Another hour or so later, I passed the only sight worth mentioning.

I had just rounded a corner when the track I was following dropped off in a sheer cliff. About two hundred feet below me was a huge mountain lake, at least a mile wide and more than twice that in length.

It was still bitterly cold, but the sky had cleared, allowing the early autumn sun to heat the surface, just enough to leave a morning mist covering the lake. Right in the middle was a small fishing boat. As I looked down at this guy with his rod over the side, it seemed as though he was on a cloud fishing for angels rather than on a lake. It was so beautiful.

Another hour passed before I finished my first lap, about twenty minutes behind what I'd been aiming for, still mumbling to Clare.

I upped my pace for the second lap, and got bored of talking to myself. Instead, I started to design my ultimate nightclub. It would've been like the big ones I'd seen in Germany, with different bars and dance floors to cater to everyone's tastes. By the time I rounded the corner at the lake, I'd redecorated the whole place twice.

Way beneath me this time, a huge blue crystal had replaced the cloud and the fisherman. The crystal was surrounded by a thin emerald green ring where it met the shore. The sun's reflection at the far end flickered like a diamond in the light of day, making this huge gem about the most beautiful sight I've ever seen. So I placed my nightclub on the banks of the lake and carried on.

As I started the third lap, I thought how nice it would be to show Clare and her kids the mountain lake. So with my nightclub ready to be opened to the public, I started to build my dream house. Soon it was going to be the mansion by the lake, the place where I'd invite Clare to join me one day.

The Sun was setting, turning the sky various shades of orange and red by the time I saw the lake again. The wind had also picked up a little, mixing the colours in an ever-changing pattern, with cresting waves moving slowly across its surface. I stood for a few moments, basking in the imaginary warmth I could feel from the lake, as if it were a comforting glowing fire.

A twinge of cramp reminded me that I didn't have all night. I looked for a spot on the mountainside to set the foundations to my house. Then I blew Clare a kiss as she sat on the balcony, bathing in the last rays of the Sun and set off up the track.

Before I started my last lap, the weather really did close in. The wind picked up first, and no matter how many corners I went around, I was walking straight into it. Then the hail started to thrash down, stinging any exposed skin or rolling down inside my jacket, and getting wedged by my Bergan in the small of my back.

If that wasn't bad enough the ground under foot was like a carpet of marbles making me stumble every few steps. Minutes ticked ever more slowly into hours, but with grit and determination, I made steady progress, then suddenly the weather cleared.

As the clouds parted and the full moon shone the way ahead, things didn't really improve for me. I was battered and bruised from the hailstorm, but worse still, my clothes were soaked. Then with a clear sky the temperature plummeted to well below freezing.

By now I'd been marching for about eighteen hours and the cold was zapping the last of my energy reserves. Each step was agonising but I kept going, thinking it was one step closer to finishing. Then I turned a corner and saw the full moon in front of me.

I stopped dead in my tracks. No matter how cold, wet and tired I was, I knew the moon should have been behind me. I spun around, and there high in the sky was the moon. I turned again, and again there was the moon, lower, but it was there too.

I couldn't work it out. No matter how many times I turned 180 degrees, the moon stayed in front of me, it was like there were two of them. I checked the time, but couldn't decide where the moon should be in the sky. Next my compass came out until I convinced myself that I'd forgotten how to use it.

I didn't know what to do as I sat down on the edge of a cliff, wondering which way up to hold the map. It wasn't the end of the world though, there were people behind me that I could follow to the finish; I just hoped it wouldn't get back to China that I managed to get lost.

Then, looking at the moon *below* me it flickered and disappeared in a gentle breeze. Slowly the lake settled and the image of the moon reformed itself on its mirror like surface. I slapped myself around the face for being so stupid, and completed the 70 km march in 19 hours 47 minutes.

I was hoping for a little better, but I was well within the cut-off time. Then, after receiving my rosette and a hot shower, a beer or ten were the only things on my mind.

About a week later, I arrived back at camp and China told me that my application for Selection had been accepted for the winter course. With a few months to go, he then suggested that I attempt a LURPs course, (Long Range Reconnaissance and Patrol), while I waited. I still had a few weeks before that started, so I took some leave, but other than more endurance training I didn't get up to much.

There is no doubt that a LURPs course is hard. Run in part by the SAS training team, it is for the very front line troops such as Pathfinders, Marines or Commandos. It starts easy enough, with some recapping of your military knowledge, followed by about ten days in the field showing off your skills.

When the test phase began, we were told that there was no definite end time; however, I knew from people I'd talked to, it would be around ten to twelve days. Then in pairs, we were dropped off in the middle of nowhere with a map, a compass and a set of coordinates we had to get to.

I was paired up with a guy from Delta Force, and moving light and fast we got to our first location in good time. Then, taking it in turns, one kept watch while the other slept until our contact arrived. Now we were given a set of tasks to do before running off to a new set of coordinates.

On our sixth night, we arrived at our location and Teddy took first watch. When he woke me up a few hours later, he said he had a bad feeling about this one. A dog team had arrived shortly after we had. They'd searched the area around the bridge he'd been watching, and then gone off in the general direction we'd come from.

There were still a few hours before our contact was due to arrive, so I took up my watch to let Teddy get some rest before the next phase started, Resistance to Interrogation.

By morning it was clear that we would be walking into a trap. Our contact arrived an hour early with a few mates, and they quickly disappeared in various directions. I woke Teddy to give him the good news.

Everybody on the course gets caught at some point, but how you get caught can mean the difference between a pass and a fail. Together, we decided to approach the area from different directions, me from the southeast and Teddy from the southwest, with a £20 bet on who could get the closest to the bridge.

I chose a route along the bank of the stream through some long reeds, getting to within twenty feet of the bridge before I ran out of cover. From there I watched the guy on the bridge for a few minutes; then, as he checked something in the Rover, I checked the time.

I was half an hour late for our meet-up, so I took a deep breath and stood up. As I did, the bush next to me shook and a bag was thrown over my head. Seconds later I was in the back of the transport, tied up like a stuffed pig. Teddy was thrown on top of me about ten minutes later. He won the bet – well, so he says anyway.

Sometime later the engine stopped and I heard the tailgate drop. Teddy was dragged out of the back of the transport; but instead of following him, I heard the tailgate close and we were off again. I tried to relax and prepare for the hell I was about to face. Around an hour later the driver stopped again and shouted that we were there.

"Sit up!" someone shouted. I didn't move, so someone pulled me up to a sitting position and my hood was taken off.

"Do you know who I am?" the guy in front of me asked.

I looked him up and down and saw a piece of white tape hanging out of his pocket. This told me he was a member of the Training Staff and had bad news for me. I'd failed.

"Yeah," I whispered.

"Boss needs a word with you," he said as he cut the plastic cuffs from my wrists. "Get cleaned up and something to eat. I'll pick you up in an hour, okay?"

When I was taken to see the Training OC a little later, he didn't really say much other than I needed to phone Adrian. Then I was taken to another room so I could have a private chat with him.

"Hi Dave, I'm sorry, but I've got some bad news,"

Adrian said softly when I finally got through.

"What's that then?" I asked, even though I had a good idea what it was going to be.

"Your Dad's dead," he answered quietly.

"Cool, I'll see you in a week or two once I've finished this course." I replied simply.

"We want you to come home now, if you can?" Adrian asked, choking back the tears.

"I'm at work, and, I'm a bit busy at the moment, so no! I'll be there in about a week. Bye." I hung up the phone and went back to see the Training OC.

He sat me down in his office, then after offering me a coffee he said, "We've arranged some transport to take you back to camp. Can you be ready by twelve?"

"I want to finish the course first, sir." I replied.

"There's no need for you too Baily. You've done okay, so, I'll propose we give you a pass under the circumstances." The OC gestured.

"But–,"

"Look Baily, you'll be doing this again anyway during Selection, and I promise it won't affect your application. So go home, your family needs you at a time like this." He assured me.

"What?" I screamed at the top of my voice. "They need me for what? To bury a fat…,"

Well, let's not get too carried away. What I said to him after that not only got me failed from the course, he also tore up my application for Selection. It must have really pissed him off, because on top of that I already knew I was going back to jail for Insubordination as soon as I got back from the funeral.

Chapter 18
Life Without . . . Dad

The family made all the arrangements for the funeral. They had asked me to help out, of course, but that got shouted abuse as an answer. Then an old pension of Dad's was cashed in and the cheque arrived in my name. I smiled as I looked at this man's worldly worth, a full £637.63. Then I laughed. I was still laughing when I went to the bank to pay the cheque in, and as I drew the cash out, I laughed even harder.

Then, when I went back to the house and threw a wad of notes across the room, while everyone was busy picking out a lovely solid oak casket. "Use that!" I laughed. I laughed hardest of all when they said the Funeral Parlour fees alone were over £800 and they didn't even have enough for that.

Then came the ultimate insult, when they said I should read from the Bible at the ceremony! In uniform, wearing the medal I'd won! For bravery! I think it goes without saying what they got. They were lucky I even turned up, although I wanted to see the body to make sure the fat git was dead. So I was there.

I thought a lot about looking for Clare while I was at home, it would have been a lot harder back then before the internet was so accessible, but, I knew roughly what area of town she was living in. Still, with Dad going to hell and me, sure I was going back to jail soon, I knew that it would have been the wrong time to try and say hello to her, so I decided against it in the end. Anyway how does a man say hello to his guardian angel?

Back on camp a few days after the funeral, I answered my charges, and by lunchtime that day I was starting a twenty-eight day jail sentence. China visited me on my second day with the good news. The Training

OC from the course I'd been on would've been taking me through the SAS Selection too. Now he'd revoke any future application from me for at least two years. I knew as soon as he said that, it really meant I'd never get an application to join the SAS passed again.

That hit me hard, and I felt myself going downhill. I knew what was coming was the reason the SAS didn't want me. But why did I always act like this when it was anything to do with Dad? Finding myself back in my bedroom hiding from everyone?

The furniture may have been different, but it was like I was twelve again, hoping Dad wouldn't open the door. But once I had got away from that life, I drove myself harder than even I had thought possible, to show everyone I was better than they were, because I hated them; because I hated Dad, and I would do anything to not turn out like him.

That had been what Dad had taught me, to hate everything about the people around me. Now that he was gone, why should I still allow him to have such a bad effect on me? With that thought, and knowing Dad would never open my door again, I allowed my hatred to die with the only man I ever truly did hate.

After that, jail was easy and I decided I wasn't going back for a while. Then at work a few weeks later, I asked China for a posting to get away from the smirks everyone carried now when they looked at me, but there wasn't anywhere to go. Still, I managed to get away on a field exercise in Poland for a few months. I had a really nice time actually.

We were covering the safety net, so we weren't part of the mock battles. Every now and again these would involve the Artillery letting off a few live rounds, and so when I visited one day, I got to meet my cartridge again. I had to let her go too, so I said my final goodbye, straight up the barrel to explode two miles away. Now that really was a good feeling, I can tell you.

Anyway, let's get back on track. Three months later, China called me into his office. "How long have you been in the Army Baily?" he asked as I took a seat.

"About ten years now Boss. Why?" I did look younger than I was.

"And you're still a B-two?" he said, talking about my trade qualification.

"Can't go on my B-one till I get my Lance-jack, can I?" I replied, knowing I needed a promotion before I could qualify to attend the course.

"Ten years and you're telling me you've never been promoted?" he said in disbelief.

"Well, I was a bit of an arse to start with Boss," I sniggered, remembering my jagged past.

He looked into it and found out I'd come off the Promotion Board two years earlier, but, the paperwork got lost in the post or something. I didn't get any back pay, but the next day I was Lance Corporal Baily.

With my promotion came a posting, and I found myself back in Germany, into the unit I had asked for. I had been told the Squadron was going to Bosnia soon; so, as I introduced myself I showed my interest in when we would be off. But apparently, goby sprogs like me, who have just got their first tape, don't go to war, they go to the Sergeant Major's office.

So off I trotted and knocked on the wrong door and got my first set of extra duties. They were a lot easier now, Two IC of the Guard. So I spent most of my time during the day sitting on the front desk answering the phone; at night it was playing PlayStation games or making coffee for the guys outside.

As I relaxed into the life I would be leading for a while, I took notice of the people who controlled it. All of them had seen me endlessly on RoP's or in jail, but they seemed to realise that their shouting wouldn't work this time, and for the most part they left me alone. Then I found out Alan was at the same unit, so I asked to be moved across to his Squadron.

I went to his sister squadron in the end, but we worked in the same garage. We also spent most of our evenings together, his marriage having not gone to plan. That had happened a few years before; I didn't ask why, so he never said. We had fun together, of course; but Alan had also found a new love, and I would one day be best man at that wedding, a job I think I did well. So we didn't have too much fun…, honest!

Alan aside, I looked at work simply as something to do. Then the dates of my trade upgrade course came through but, before we could go, all those on the course had to sit a mock exam to make sure they made the grade. So ten minutes after picking up my pen I walked out with a pass mark in the high nineties. Half the class failed, and needed extra Maths.

I was told it would be a good re-cap for me so I should sit in on the lessons. Then after our Maths teacher got almost every equation we would need to know wrong, I stood up and gave the lesson for him. Again, during electrical theory, I had to finish it off for him before these guys failed again. Bet you'll never guess who the named instructor was for the practical lesson!

After all that, they said I couldn't go on the course because they needed me to get the next lot ready to go first. I told them I'd sign off and get out the Army if they did that, so they changed their minds.

Back on a training camp for a few months, I met a few of the guys from Bosnia. Knowing how hard I worked out there, and having read some of my training records, I asked them about becoming an instructor. There were ways and means of doing it, of course, but I'd need to make Sergeant first. At the rate my promotions were coming, that would've taken about thirty years, so I gave up on the idea.

Back at the Regiment in Germany, after passing my

upgrade with flying colours, I started to relax back into normal Army life, which was probably the worst thing I could've done. The years of running around like a lunatic had taken their toll on my body, but with the constant training my muscles had held me together. Now, as I relaxed, so did they, and the niggling pains started.

The doctor offered half a dozen operations, for this tendon and that cartilage, to help relieve the pain. By then though I'd already been under the knife eleven times, and other than the sick leave I would've been entitled to, I couldn't see any benefit in it. I turned him down.

A few months passed then there was an attack in Kosovo and the unit was put on high alert. Inspections galore started, as all the equipment was made ready, and soon we're out practicing deployments every few days. A few weeks later, the situation was no better and the CO called the whole unit onto parade.

"There seems to be little doubt that we will be sending people to Kosovo, we just don't know when," came over the PA system set up for the CO's speech.

"When we do get the call, you need to be aware that at the moment, the Russians are currently exactly where we want to be. Negotiations have started well, but in case they break down we are forming an advance party to set up for a full deployment." The CO continued.

"Now make no mistake, ladies and gentlemen, if we have to fight our way in, we will, and people will die. So think about your family, and your loved ones, but never forget about your training, because that's what will bring you back home, alive." He finished, before we were dismissed to our troops for a more detailed briefing.

It was a wake-up call for the whole unit. This was going to be a major deployment, so it would come in three stages; and this was the end of stage one: the mad panic. It's the first part of every plan: the Army gets everything they've got out there as quick as possible and sort out the mess later.

Then, as the situation becomes clearer we move into stage two and a refined plan is put into place: a deployment taking what you need, to where you need it. But moving ten thousand men with equipment, to a country that's virtually landlocked is a logistical nightmare, so you need advanced coms to help keep control.

Now with no one sure of the Russians' intentions, those advance coms would deploy with the beachheads, calling in air support. Then once we have a foothold it's onto stage three, and get everybody else in, quick.

We didn't really have a problem with the Russians at the time, and thinking they would give in within a few days the Regiment practised the new deployment plan with a short exercise. When we came back in, I found my name near the top of the list for the Advance Party.

With updated information coming out at our next briefing, we were told that the area assigned to us was key to the whole deployment, and that the Russians didn't want to give it up as easily as other locations. Talks were still going on, but we were to train for the worst: to take the area from a squadron of heavily fortified Spetsnaz: the Russian Special Forces!

Our primary mission was communications, so that's where the main part of our training focused, setting up the equipment in ever quicker times. Secondary to that was defending our location, where I would play a major part in setting traps and funnel-necks, to focus any enemy advance onto a defended area. But with casualties also expected on the front line, we needed to be able to replace them, and infantry training became intense.

We really were expecting the call any day now, to fly into an airport and possibly take it by force. So we were on and off helicopters with explosions going off all around us. Then I'm in and out of buildings, practicing how to clear hangers, while live fire exercises happened every few days. This training really was as close to being in a battle as it gets. I know, I've been in one. Then the call comes in: are we going?

"Right lads," the Advance party OC said. "The Russians have given into negotiations, and the Division has already moved in, so you're all stood down. We will however be sending a small fatigue party over to help with their initial set-up. If your name's on the list outside, report back in here. The rest of you, two weeks leave and back to your troops. Away you go!"

One hundred and twenty-six people walked out of that room. On the list were twenty-one names of married men, all with young children; I was among the ninety-three people that signed off that day. It was the largest number of Sign Offs, in a single day, a regiment in the British Army has ever had.

Everyone had his or her own reason, and as I walked to the Admin office I thought of mine. We had trained for the worst-case scenario and were ready for it, but with the negotiations making steady progress, it had started to look like it would be a peaceful handover; so a battle had become less likely.

That wasn't what we were going there for anyway. We'd be staying to do what the Royal Corps of Signals do for a living, and keep the messages flowing. The part I played in that, by keeping the generators in tiptop condition, I was very good at and enjoyed doing.

In Kosovo I would have been left alone to do my work, but back here on camp, every Monday morning would start with the words, "Stand by your beds, locker inspection in ten minutes." Then I'd get shouted at for the next three hours for having dirty washing in my laundry basket.

What with that, and all the menial tasks that were

given out simply because your troop Staffy got out of the wrong side of his bed, I'd had enough. I was thirty, not thirteen, and had proved myself as both a soldier and a tradesman. So if there wasn't a job for me to do in the Army, then it was time to prove I was a man. It was time to go home.

When you 'Sign Off,' you've effectively handed in your notice at work, and in the Army the process can take up to a year, so you're supposed to have an interview with the CO within two weeks, the same time-frame you have to change your mind.

His list was so long it took nearly six weeks to get to me. By then, the only thing that would have kept me in would have been an offer of a deployment. When he offered me the simple choice to stay in the unit, I declined to change my mind.

Alan thought I was stupid, and looking back, I was. If I'd waited another six months I would've got a better pension. Nonetheless, I stuck to my guns, and a few weeks after my CO's interview I got a letter with my discharge date. With time taken off for leave and resettlement, I had about five months left in Germany.

I could've asked for a posting back to the UK, but I couldn't be bothered with the grief of starting at a new unit. Still, I went on a load of resettlement courses designed to help me get a decent job. I did a fair few guard duties too, but they were nothing to write home about. So my last few months dragged on until about a week before I was due to leave.

The Sergeant Major came into my room on his Monday morning inspection. On my windowsill was a hip flask that Staff Hammond and Zed Foster had given me as a leaving present. The Sergeant Major picked it up, and, after sniffing the contents, poured the neat whisky out of the window. Then he warned me for Orders, Alcohol in the Block.

I know I swore never to accept a drink from the men who gave me that flask, but that wasn't the point. It was my whisky, and I wanted to do that! I didn't play up though, if that's what you're thinking. I got a £100 fine ten minutes before I handed my uniform back in.

My ferry wasn't till the following day, so I had a few cans talking about old times with a guy in my troop. Then we decided to take it outside onto a grass bank next to the accommodation block. Out in the sunshine, a few of the lads were heading back in for a shower after football or whatever.

"What's going on here then?" one of them asked.

"Dave's last day in the green, mate," the lad I was with answered.

"What? You're joking, right?" he said, a little surprised.

"Yep, this time tomorrow I'll be in a pub as Mr Baily," I told him happily enough.

"Stay there. I've got a crate in my room," the footballer said, and off he trotted to get more beer.

An hour later, the twenty people that had joined us decided we needed some music, so a stereo and a fridge appeared. Then there wasn't enough to go round for the fifty or so that turned up later still; so, as they arrived, so did the barbecue and a barrel. Then I was amazed, as the number swelled into the hundreds, to hear so many of them say; they had felt safe knowing I had been fighting beside them.

And I left the Army as I had joined it – a soldier to the last.

Chapter 19
Life Without . . . the Army

I bummed around for a while when I got back to the UK. It wasn't because I really wanted to – it was the fact that I was over-qualified that prevented me from getting a job. They probably thought I wanted too much money, or more likely, their positions. I would have unblocked the toilets if they'd asked me to; I just wanted to earn a living.

Oh well, I still had my Army pay out to fall back on you're thinking. Well I invested that in a small company didn't I, then it all went Pete Tong, so I lost the lot. Feeling like I couldn't get any lower, I hit the bottle with every spare penny I had. Then it's amazing how quick those debts add up, isn't it?

Less than six months after leaving the Army, I had to move back in with Mum, because I couldn't afford the rent on my flat. Don't get me wrong, bridges had been built with all my family, and even Mum says they were some of the best times of her life. But as I waited for the lift each morning, leaving for the Job Centre, I could see the field where Andy died.

I did get a job eventually, so I was soon zipping around the country looking after till systems on various holiday camp sites. The job was fairly low paid, but it had the advantage of a company car, and I got in-touch with Alan to see what he was up to.

He'd been out of the Army for a while by then himself, and settled down with his new wife somewhere in Yorkshire. Luck would have it that I had some work coming up in his area so, I arranged to stay nearby for a couple of weeks.

Over the first few days I was around, we caught up on what we had each been doing since we'd last met, and then Alan said I should have a chat with his boss. So the following weekend we got together again, this time with his boss, and met in a local pub.

As the night went on Alan's boss asked if I was looking for work in the area. Really I wasn't, but, when he said that he could probably double my wage, I changed my mind. He went on to tell me he was looking for another electrician to become Alan's team mate, and then talked more about what I'd actually be doing.

The job itself sounded fantastic and not too different to what I did in the Army, just now, I'd be fixing machines inside a factory, rather than generators in the rain. Eventually after some encouragement from Alan, and a few too many beers, I agreed to an interview.

Other than turning up on time the following week, my interview was terrible. The size of the factory was daunting, so, when they handed me a basic test that I had to fill out, I forgot what two plus two equalled and wrote down five. Then I didn't finish my practical assessment because I was taking too long, so, by the time I met the Managing Director I'd given up on getting the job.

After another half an hour of me mumbling about myself I shook hands with everyone, feeling quite relieved that I enjoyed the job I already had, and said my goodbyes'. When I got to my car less than two minutes later I answered my mobile phone, and. the Managing Director introduced himself again.

"I've had a word with the Engineering Manager Mr Baily," he said, referring to Alan's boss, "and well, we think we've come to a decision already. When can you start?"

Regardless of how my interview went I was expecting it to take at least a week to hear anything; I dropped my phone from the shock. Thankfully it was still working when I picked it up again a few moments later. This was a huge decision for me to take, so I asked for a few hours to think it over, promising to contact him the following morning.

Having already booked the day off, I went back to my hotel and sat in the bar. By the time Alan had finished work I still hadn't made up my mind and he joined me.

"Why are you even thinking about this? Compared to what we use to do in the Army, this jobs' a doddle mate." he told me.

"It's not about the job Al, but how do I get there when I give the company their car back?" I said seeing a bigger picture.

"Well that's easy, I'll pick you up." He laughed, but forgetting one minor fact.

"I live two hundred miles away." I reminded him of it.

"Don't be stupid, you'll be moving up here, right?" Alan said, and ordered another round of drinks.

"With what? Anywhere I find is going to ask for three months' rent in advance. I just haven't got that kind of money mate." I replied, knowing there was no way I could actually take the job.

"Is that all it is, the money?" Alan said, gesturing me to come closer, "Don't tell the misses but, I've got some put by, we'll sort it. Now give them a call."

I took a deep breath and phoned my boss to hand in my notice. The following morning I arranged the start date for my new role, and true to his word, Alan helped me find everything I needed.

At work I soon proved that my poor interview was only down to nerves and started to impress everyone. The main thing I really had to learn was that what the Army had taught me, though right for a combat situation, was completely wrong for a factory. But with Alan by my side, having already learnt that lesson, within three months my skills were only matched by his own.

Over the next two years or so, I worked hard and was rewarded with qualification after qualification; until we all turned up one morning to the news that the factory was closing. The company was very supportive though, and with nearly two thousand people suddenly looking for work, there was many of them that needed help.

I had the opportunity to work with Alan again after we were made redundant, but I suppose I felt that I would always be working in his shadow if I did, so, I opted for another offer I had on the table instead. After that I became very focused on my career, going from strength to strength with every contract I worked on.

Other things happened too of course, as I had a couple of failed attempts to find Miss Right, but I suppose I'm not the settling type. I also became a Godfather several times over, each of them holds a special place in my heart, so I don't want to only focus on one here. Needless to say that life in Yorkshire was fantastic for another four or five years. Then I got an email about another job opening.

The company I was working for at the time had won a major contract, and needed to expand quickly, so they were looking for volunteers to help set up a new office. When I asked for some more details, it seemed like a good chance for me to get on the management ladder. The only downside was that I would be covering the Home Counties. Really I should have taken longer to think it over, but blinded by my career I said I'd help out.

Within a week of accepting my new role I was living out of a bag, staying in a different hotel each night. I wish I could have carried on like that but it was costing an absolute fortune, so I had to find somewhere a little more permanent to live.

Again I should have thought for longer but, with Bedfordshire right in the centre of the area I covered, it seemed logical to look for a flat there. But within a fortnight, I knew that moving back to my hometown was a big mistake.

All of my family had moved away by then, so, in a hope to make some friends I went to the pub on a rare day off. It all started very nice with a lovely home cooked lunch before, I got chatting to a few of the locals. Then a little later, I introduced myself to a couple of guys playing pool.

"I think I remember you. Which high school did you go to?" One of them asked.

After he recognised the name of one of the schools I went to, he then laughed and joked about how he had bullied me there. An hour later I'd had enough and punched him. People were splitting us apart before any real fight broke out, but thankfully, they'd seen these guys winding me up, so I wasn't in any trouble. Still it could have gone better.

On a better note, I found out Clare lived nearby and after getting in touch over Facebook, she accepted an offer to go out to dinner.

"So tell me everything?" she asked across the table, in the candle light.

I looked across the table, into the eyes of my childhood nurse, full of love and tenderness. Then I saw the face of my guardian angel, the beauty within, that held me together in a world of horrors. And now I was looking at the woman she had become.

She was my inspiration and my guiding light through Bosnia. She was my drive and my focus whenever I trained. Everything I've ever done, every achievement that I've made, it was all for her. *Clare is everything to me.*

I never could find a way to tell her that though. In the end my feelings for her put such a strain on our friendship we fell out. I have no-one to blame but myself, and now I also had no reason to stay in Bedfordshire. The only thing that held me back was my depleted bank account.

I started to work a lot of overtime to help rebuild my funds. Then after about a month of hard graft my shoulder started to ache continually. Not just at work either. Sometimes at night, the pain would get so bad I couldn't sleep, so I registered with a doctor and booked myself in.

He couldn't really find much wrong with me at first, so suggested I try some physiotherapy to help relieve the pain. I was back the following week in agony when it didn't. Another month passed until the results of an MRI scan came back, then the doctor asked about my car crash, and pointed to four damaged vertebrae in my neck.

I told him that I've never had a car crash, well, not a serious one anyway. In fact I think I broke my neck during my first few weeks in Bosnia. I was use to sleeping on a double bed back on camp, so when I rolled over on the top bunk, well, I ran out of mattress. My face hit the floor, but my feet didn't.

The doctor went on to tell me that there wasn't anything that needed to be done about the vertebrae themselves, but; the disc between two of them had slipped towards my spinal cord and was slowly paralysing me. There was an operation they could do to remove the damaged disc, and it had a good success rate, so I suppose there was light at the end of the tunnel. Then after advising me that I'd be dead in a month if he didn't, he signed me off work indefinitely.

Anywhere else in the country I might have been okay, but stuck in my hometown, with absolutely no friends, and after kick-starting my childhood memories. I gave myself about a week.

I took the doctor's advice of course, and the following day I gave my boss the good news. Then, while I waited for an appointment with a specialist, I saw what I could find out about the operation I was likely to have.

My injuries are much the same as whiplash so, it was a much more common operation than I thought it would be. The procedure itself is pretty gruesome, and as with all surgery it carried risks. But on the good side, if it was successful, I should be fully recovered in around ten weeks.

As the days of waiting for my appointment with the specialist turned into weeks, it was clear to me that I wouldn't make it back to work before my full sick pay ran out. I didn't have any kind of insurance for this type of thing, so, I started to phone around, working out my incomings and out goings.

Everyone I spoke to was very polite as they reminded me that I'd had to renew all my contracts when I moved, and I was tied into that amount for twelve months, so they couldn't help. Then after I was told that technically I was still employed, so, only 80% of my rent would be paid by housing benefits, I had my budget.

Just for the basics of life, gas, electric, water and the rest of the rent, I would still need to find another £30 per month before I could even think about buying food. My situation didn't get any better when I finally got my appointment. With two months to wait before seeing the specialist, I'd now be seeing him just as my full sick pay stopped.

There wasn't much I could do except wait for my appointment, and for the most part I did okay. With a better idea now of when I might be back at work, I had another try with my creditors. Though some still wouldn't budge on reducing my payments for a few months, most were a little more understanding, so I managed to make a few cutbacks. It wasn't much, and things would still fall apart before I got back to work, but it gave me some valuable breathing space.

Time dragged on until I finally met the specialist at the hospital. He was very business-like as he carried out his examination, and after I described the progression of my symptoms, he confirmed that I needed surgery. Then taking a piece of metal off his desk, he went on and described how he was going to insert it into my spine.

It was nothing that I hadn't read or seen on the internet so I relaxed and asked, "So when are you free?" He checked through his diary and booked me in two months later.

I could have broken down in tears in his office. I had stretched my money as far as it would go. There wasn't anything left to sell, no more favours I could ask, within the next few weeks I was going to be living on a negative budget. I'd be lucky to survive until the operation, let alone the three months I'd need afterwards.

By the time I got home I'd managed to get myself into a real state, wondering how I ever thought I could have been happy in that godforsaken town. That night, the nightmares of my terrorised childhood started.

Now I knew I was in trouble: having to relax so my neck doesn't get any worse, all the other niggling pains have already started again. My knees and ankles had got so bad that just getting out of bed is agony, let alone walking to the shops for some food. And when I do make it there, I can't feel my right arm, so I fumble with everything I pick up. Then I start thinking someone's going to see me struggling and want to mug me for my last few quid. Terrified of going out, I stayed in my room as much as possible.

I was in my room with a bed I couldn't get out of because of the pain. I was in my room with a dining chair, the only piece of furniture I found comfortable to sit on. I was in my room hiding from everyone who might hurt me, and I had no way out. Was I in my room or in my hell?

The longer it went on, the worse I got. Soon I couldn't tell the difference between day and night, keeping the curtains closed so the debt collectors would think I was out. Then my mobile phone gets nicked, but, the insurance hasn't been paid, so they won't pay out. And after the TV package and broadband get cut off, I'm alone.

With my mind locked somewhere in my childhood; life didn't make sense anymore. Each day I'd try to forget the dream I'd just woken from to be reminded of the true horrors I faced when I slept again. The real bad stuff that no publisher would let me tell you about, but, I had to tell someone, anyone; even if I was the only person around. So I wrote down my nightmares and tried to put some order to the chaos. It didn't really help matters.

I hadn't eaten or slept properly for weeks when my computer screen popped up with a reminder that my housing benefit was due. I also knew from the date that I was due to have the operation so, I drew out as much cash as I could before the banks transferred it, and tried to work out some kind of budget.

Over half the cash I had would be spent the following day getting to the hospital. Then, allowing for my expected prescription charges I had £7 left. What was the point of even trying? It was another three weeks before I would get any more money.

On top of that I was already dangerously underweight, so there was I higher risk of something going wrong during the operation; but in all likelihood I'd pull through and slowly starve to death in pain, or, I could speed up the process and jump off the nearest bridge.

I walked into the bathroom for some toilet roll. Catching my reflection in the mirror I went for a closer look. Even with a six-week-old beard disguising my face, I could see how drawn and gaunt I'd become from the weight loss. Over my body it was even more apparent, seeing my skeleton rather than any kind of definition.

"What the fuck are you doing to yourself?" I asked, looking into my own dead eyes for the answer. "You have never quit anything in your life, now fight!'

There wasn't any voices from my past, this was me speaking, but images of my Army career came flooding back, the good times and the hard. It was the one consistent throughout my whole life that I could hold on to. Through hardship, loss and injury, I fought back. Then if people tried to put me down, I'd lash out and put them in hospital; when they said I couldn't do something, I trained until I could; and when they ran in fear; I stood my ground.

I wasn't having an epiphany but I realised that I couldn't do everything at once. For now I couldn't do anything until after my operation, so, I got cleaned up and packed the few things I needed.

I knew that I had to keep my mind off childhood, but the operation held no fear to me. This was my thirteenth time now, but that was just a number too. Instead I found myself fumbling the golden gloves I'd won in the Army, hanging around my neck, and thought about the night I'd won them. That night I proved to four thousand people that I could fight, tomorrow I only had to prove it to one.

Having to leave in the early hours to make my appointment I didn't even try to sleep, so I must have looked in a real state when I arrived at the hospital, but I was ready for anything. More importantly I was relaxed and focused on what was going on around me.

My tests came back clear and soon after arriving I was shown to a bed. Then a little later, a nurse arrived with some tablets for me to take. As she was doing some final checks, I dozed off to sleep.

"Ark at you." I heard her say and opened my eyes to look across at her.

"Sorry to wake you Mr Baily, but just so you know

your blood pressure is fine. Your oxygen level is a little low, but nothing to worry about, I just need to let the anaesthetist know about it. Now do you have any questions before I go?" she asked.

"What time does the doctor to his rounds in the morning?" I asked.

"Oh, normally about seven I think, they'll know better up at the ward." She told me.

"Can you book me a taxi for ten past please…, think I've left the iron on?" I said, with a grin.

She laughed, "There's a phone in the lobby in case he's running late. Now, normally I'd be telling people to relax, but the anaesthetist may need a word with you. He'll only be a few minutes so do you think you can stay awake that long?"

"Sorry, it's been a long day," I smiled, and tried not to relax. It didn't work because the next thing I remember is someone demanding for me to open my eyes.

"Mr Baily, can you open your eyes for me please." The voice went again.

The drugs where taking their toll, so I couldn't remember how to open my eyes. "In or out?" I screamed.

"You're coming out. Everything went as planned, I just need you to open your eyes."

I flung my hand across to feel where the wound should have been on my neck, but I couldn't tell if my arm had even moved.

"I don't want you to do that, just your eyes, can you open them Mr Baily." The voice went.

I sat up and opened my eyes to a blur.

"Very good, I just need to check your eyes."

Blinding flashes but my vision cleared. Blurs turned into people in white coats, and soon, I could make out my own legs. As I looked, each foot moved the way I expected it to, then again with my hands.

"Get that thing out of me before I wake up again!" I

demanded, indicating towards the catheter tube still doing its job.

Laughs, followed by the voice, "He's alright, take him straight to the ward please." I relaxed and drifted back into darkness.

I was screaming when I came round again a few hours later, this time to the tea lady. Once I realised where I was, I made my apologies for swearing, asking politely if I was allowed a drink. After checking she came back saying I needed to wait until after visiting hours, and I was reminded why I hate hospitals.

I had already noticed the ward was full, and soon they would all be moaning about how much pain they were still in. Then if anyone felt sorry for the poor guy who didn't get a visitor, I'd probably break down, adding years to my own healing process. I had to get out of there.

I seem to have a high tolerance to both pain and drugs, which I put to the test, as the tea lady left the ward, by sitting up. The movement itself was excruciating but, once my head was directly above my shoulders, it soon became more comfortable than laying down. Trying my movements again, my head and neck were very stiff and painful, but everything seemed to work okay.

I knew I wouldn't be going anywhere for a while at least, but to stay seated the way I was, meant one of two things, both meant getting out of bed. Using the frame for support I stumbled to the controls for the bed, but, they were written in Egyptian hieroglyphics, I gave up and headed for the chair instead.

I dozed off a few times before the surgeon did his rounds that evening. He confirmed everything went okay by describing my operation as "boring". Then went on to tell me that things were looking good for me and I could hope to be out after the weekend.

The nurse was on her rounds soon after the surgeon,

telling me all my vitals were low and the doctor wanted me back in bed. I humoured her by getting back onto the bed while she checked the others. Once she turned her back, I found my dressing gown and headed for the door.

As I slowly walked down the corridor, I shook my head. I knew I was on the verge of a nervous breakdown any day now, but, I didn't want to lose my mind in public.

Knowing the part of the hospital that I was in I headed for the shop. But still having ten minutes to wait for it to open, I carried on past and outside into the grounds, and the cool air helped clear my head.

Reason would say it was still the Thursday that I had booked in; that meant a three or four-day stay. I was hoping for shorter but there was nothing I could do about that. I did consider discharging myself over the weekend once I felt strong enough, but without the doctors blessing it would just be another thing for me to contend with.

A gust of wind told me my senses were coming back, and that I was still only wearing my surgical gown. After checking I had some money, I went back to the shop and brought as much milk, fruit juice and sweets as I could carry. Then as I walked back into the ward with my treats the Matron stared at me from her desk.

"Sorry, I was looking for the shower but forgot where I put my clothes." I offered with a smile.

"They're in the locker by your bed, and that's where I want to have you in five minutes Mr Baily." She said smiling back.

"Yes ma'am, but please be gentle, I've only just had surgery." I said, giving her the best wink I could.

It took her a few seconds to catch up, and, a little embarrassed she pointed in the direction of the ward.

Still smiling when I got to my bed, I changed into my own clothes, just as the visitors started to arrive, and I pulled out my laptop. My priority now was to tell work

I'd had the op. After surgery like this getting my old job back was my only chance of work so, I needed to know how long they'd hold it open for me.

Logging onto the hospitals internet I checked my emails first and read, 'Wage payment error' in the subject line of one of them. I dreaded opening it thinking that I owed the company money but, after reading through it several times, I eventually worked out the error was in my favour. Logging onto my bank moments later I saw that I had over £700 available funds.

"At last, a break." I said aloud, letting out a sigh of relief.

The money wasn't just a break; it was my saving grace. Even if I couldn't get to a bank until Monday I could still get my hands on nearly all of that. Proper budgeting might have seen it last for several months, but realistically I gave it two. Through that time my cash would get topped up with sick pay and benefits, so, things were actually looking good for a change.

A little later, I went onto Facebook and updated my status, so people would know I was okay, adding a photo of my latest war wound. Replying to a few personal messages of support I'd received since my last post, I noticed all but two were from strangers, but my spirits lifted a little more.

The simple message from Mum was the most poignant, because I know her offer to visit was genuine. She is getting on in years now, and I understood she couldn't cope with the journey, so I tried to stay positive in my reply; but it felt more like I was saying goodbye.

I've had a very turbulent relationship over the years with Mum, and said many harsh things to her. But the one thing she has always been is Mum. She saw me throw my crutches aside, when I passed basic training, and was as proud as any parent would be. Travelling to Germany alone, she visited me after I broke my leg, and, she is the only person in my family to visit my home. I love her for that.

But I could only hold myself together for a limited time, and, when I finally broke I would be back in childhood. There she's the bitch that abandoned me, the one that wouldn't believe her own son. Mum, in my childhood, started this whole thing. And I hate her for that.

Emotions welled up inside me and tears started to flow down my cheeks like rivers. Going to the toilet for privacy I regained control after a few minutes and cleaned myself up.

When I came out the ward was still full of visitors, so, grabbing my jacket I headed for the exit again. The cold air refreshed me once again, and slowly, I convinced myself the money in the bank was going to solve all of my troubles and more. With the spare cash I would even treat myself to a day off being poor when I got home.

I knew I wouldn't be able to do much, but, maybe a movie and a pint might do me some good. If I kept it up, I might even be able to hold off my memories, until I get the all clear to go back to work. Do that and I would be fine, work would consume me, and childhood has no place there.

A lot happier I went back to the ward, just as the last of the visitors were leaving. Then getting comfortable on my bed I gorged myself on the junk food my body was now craving, and settled in for the long night ahead.

My sleeping patterns are erratic when I'm in the best of health. Today, I had taken my pre-meds at ten that morning, and been in and out of sleep since. Anyone I asked would say that was drug induced sleep, and now my body needed a natural rest to help it recover.

Whether that's true or not, I don't know, but I have never been able to sleep the first night after an operation.

Passing the time I played a few games on Facebook until a chat box opened. Seeing it was from Zoe I replied to her brief message and we started chatting.

I've known Zoe for years but only ever online, so having never met in the flesh, so to speak, she is hard to describe. That doesn't matter right now though, we have a very close and intimate relationship, with few secrets' kept between us. She also knew I was hurting from more than just my physical injuries, guessing my past had something to do with that; but for now she gave me what I needed, company.

We chatted until the early hours before my second dose of sleeping tablets took their toll. Nonetheless, I was awake early the next morning and feeling much better. After a shower I had no trouble pulling a polo neck sweater over my head. My stats had also returned to normal and I had even refused to take any pain relief drugs.

The surgeon was obviously impressed with my early recovery when he did his rounds that day, so I tried my luck and asked about going home. He took a few moments to confer with the junior doctors following him about.

I didn't understand all the jargon they went on about, but they were all in agreement that there was nothing more for me to gain by staying in hospital. My taxi to the train station arrived twenty-three hours after I'd had surgery.

I asked the driver to find a cashpoint first, and with hard cash in my pocket changed my destination to home. The ride cost a fortune but everything was looking positive for me.

Even with the added expense of the fare I had enough money in my pocket to last to my review in six weeks' time. In the morning I was going to empty my bank account, adding a little luxury to lift my spirits, and if I could arrive at the review smiling, I could be back at work a month later.

True, my rent arrears would get worse, and the debt collectors would still be banning at my door every few days. But they couldn't take what I didn't have, and I knew I couldn't get evicted in my condition.

It seemed like such a long time but I knew as each minute passed I was getting closer to going back to work. Living for today and thinking no further than waking up tomorrow and living again, it was achievable.

Then in two months, three at the outside, my income would change from £400 in benefits, to well over £2000 in wages. I know money doesn't solve all of life's problems, but with 90% of them taken care of the rest don't seem to matter anymore.

Chapter 20

The driver indicated we were near home, and with a few directions he parked outside my flat. Walking through the door I kicked the mess aside to make a path for myself and sat down. Looking around the rubbish dump I called home brought me down straight away so, I knew I had to change that first.

The clean-up started well, and as I went along I had a touch of OCD, so it took a few days to go through everything. I made it out shopping a few times, filling my freezer and cupboards with food. I also brought an internet dongle and passed the time on Facebook games or chatting to Zoe. Then, after a message from Lee, I added a cheap pay-and-go phone and had voice contact with a friend.

I was still having nightmares most times I slept but, managing to keep myself occupied while I was awake, I seemed to be keeping on track. Then I had a hic-up on the way back from having my staples out.

I'm not sure what brought it on but, suddenly, flashes of my past were in front of my eyes and I had to be alone. I had done the right thing though, because walking into my clean and tidy home, I felt safe.

Soon my breathing calmed down bringing the here and now back into focus. I was thinking of heading out again for the last few bits I needed when Lee called. With it still fresh in my mind, I said I'd just had a flashback, though I was okay now. Instantly concerned, he offered for me to stay with him for a few days. My refusals fell on deaf ears, so, after Lee brought me a train ticket I left early the next morning.

I've never really lost contact with Lee, though visits were rare; my last had been several years before when I became Godfather to his youngest. Seeing her sitting on the backseat of the car with her older sibling, when Lee picked me up,

I turned to him and said. "Wish you'd told me, I would've left it a few days." pointing to the smiling faces behind us.

"Be alright mate, they're going back to mum tomorrow, then we can party." He said, telling me plans for a night on the town.

My Goddaughter was at that inquisitive age, so she wanted to know everything about me when we got back to Lee's house. After answering her many questions I was eventually accepted into the family fold, and she went about making sure I knew everyone's name.

"And this is my Daddy. You can call him Lee because he's not your Daddy." She proudly announced. "Where's your Daddy Uncle Dave?" The sweetest of questions from the innocence of childhood.

I snapped. Every door in my mind opened, every wall crumbled to ash. I lowered my voice and told her. "My Daddy's exactly where he should be."

"Has he gone to heaven like my goldfish?" she asked feeling sad.

I had forgotten who I was, but I knew who she was, and anything I said now was not for her tender ears. Covering my mouth so nothing could slip out, I just stared at her. This was my Goddaughter and I had to protect her, from me.

"Leave your Uncle Dave alone, now out, the both of you." Lee said ushering the kids outside to join their friends.

Childhood wasn't the worst time of my life, it's not even close to it, but it was constant, violent, and I was too young to understand it. I was punished daily, sometime several times, the painful lessons teaching me just one thing, people were violent. Starving and in agony I was then set to work or out to fight bullies. This was normal life for me and with it Kelly took my fear, and Dad took my morality.

When I joined the Army, they didn't want those things. They wanted aggression without morals, they wanted endurance without limits; they needed men who would walk into a hail of bullets without fear of death. They wanted people like me to fight back. Training gave me the strength I needed, with practice, I became lethal with it.

Discipline gave me ultimate control, but my childhood masks that control. While I was like this, I was an abused kid that wanted revenge; and soon I would have the strength to take it, on anyone. Now I was just like Dad, and I would die before I'd let that happen.

I was aware of my surroundings but they were a dream. For the rest of the day I don't remember saying anything, I don't think I even moved until after the kids had long been in bed. Even then I only recall moving to the sofa, though I'm sure I would've talked to Lee at some point. Again the following day I stayed in the background, a shell of a body in a dream world.

I knew we had dropped the kids back with their mum and were driving back when I turned to Lee and said, "Sorry I'm like this mate, did I do anything to upset the kids?"

"Nar bud, they were glad to see you. So what's up?" he asked, putting some of my fears to rest.

"My head's fucked, I just need to get home mate. Can you drop me at the station?" I replied, trying to hide my face from the world with my hands.

"Okay mate, but what's up anyway, Bosnia?" Lee fished for what I was thinking about.

"Bosnia? What the fuck could your daughter say to remind me of Bosnia?" I screamed, shocking Lee into a swerve.

"Whoa, calm down mate, she didn't mean anything." Lee said, quickly regaining control of the car.

"I know, it's not her fault," I replied calming back down, "Just if she'd carried on pushing about my old man I'd have told her; he was a fat, vicious bastard that beat the shit out of me from when I was six years old. That's something no kid her age should hear."

"Shit the bed, so you going to speak to the police about it?" Lee suggested.

You have to understand here that I have never spoken of my childhood since leaving it, I've only written about it. Lee had little cause to read anything I wrote in the Army so, this was a complete shock to him.

"And what the fuck are they going to do? Dig him up? Well they can't, because they burned him and I watched, and they hate me for that, all of them!" I shouted suddenly angry again.

"Get it together man, you're not making any sense. Now I'm here to listen, so tell me, who got burnt; who hates you?" Lee said, trying not to trigger me off again.

"They all do, my whole fucking family. Watch me get tortured will you, fuckers! Oh, you must have dreamt it. Well I'll show them who they decided to fuck with, and fuck cares what happens." I growled through gritted teeth, my emotions wreaking havoc.

"Dave, you're really not making any sense. Now take a deep breath and tell me what the hell is going on." Lee asked as he pulled the car into a layby.

"Sorry mate, I love you as though you were my brother, but I can't do this with you. I'm really sorry if I upset the kids but do me a favour, drop me at the station." I begged, tears welling up in my eyes.

"You ain't going anywhere until I know you won't do something stupid. Now what's all this about when you were a kid? You've never told me any of this before." Lee put his hand on my shoulder, keeping me with him.

I looked up at him with tears in my eyes, "Why would I mate? Would you really have been interested in the battered kid that couldn't fight?"

"Dave, you're not a battered kid who couldn't fight. You're my mate, and I've seen you fight, it's terrifying. Now how about we sack the town tonight and get a few beers in. I'll even see if I can find my old chess board. How's that sound?" He smiled encouragingly, gently shaking my shoulder.

I could see that he meant what he said and nodded before and we set off again. Then stocking up with beer we carried onto Lee's house.

With over eighteen years of armed service between us, both Lee and I have deep scars from those times. He didn't push too hard about my childhood, though I did offer for him to read some of my recent writings. Seeing his face as he read about the way a father treated a child, the same age as his own, I think he understood why I didn't want to talk to him.

Childhood aside for a moment, much of what I went through in the Army Lee had been there with me, going through the event itself, and my friends also being his, he suffered too.

A few days later, I realised I was losing my mind when Lee dropped me off at the station. As his car pulled away the world about me turned into a dream state again, my body going through the motions of life, but, somehow, I wasn't in control of it. Tickets were shown and changes were made until I got to my front door.

Stopping, I prayed aloud. "Now I will walk into the valley with the shadow of death about me and I will fear nothing!"

As I spoke I crossed the threshold, then the Padre's words came to mind: *"If we're going to do this, we're going to do it right, and you will soldier on,"* and I focused on how to turn my Life Without... into a published book.

I thought it would be easy at first. I already had a lot of my nightmares written on my laptop so; I just put them in some kind of order and send them to a publisher to do the rest, right?

The reply I got telling me not to bother them again with such drivel wasn't very polite. After I'd read it I slammed my fist down onto my laptop so hard it bounced off the table and the screen went blank.

I tried everything I knew to bring my laptop back to life but it was no good, it was dead, and, it felt like my whole life had died with it. Even if I somehow could get hold of another computer I'd need to re-write everything. I just didn't know if I had the strength for that.

Still, I scoured the local second hand shops, and eating heavily into the money I had left, settled on the cheapest laptop I could find. Then looking at the blank page on the screen when I unpacked it I cried.

I knew now if I was ever going to write my memoirs, I would have to write about them in order. The only other time I'd even attempted that was in Bosnia so, I think I also knew I wasn't just risking my sanity, I was risking my very life. But I also knew I had to get this off of my chest before my review in less than four weeks' time.

Once again immersed in my childhood, with its deepest secrets now unlocked, I hit my lowest point. But within the chaos I found some pivotal points to focus on, reliving them over and over again.

Each I wrote down, and each I'd read over and over, only to relive the memory again and again. Then with each edit I did, the rambling abuse slowly turned into a story, and each time I understood a little more about myself.

In the early days I was only going to write about my childhood, so, within three weeks I had a first draft manuscript. I knew from the publishers comments in his email that I still had a lot of work to do. But I wanted to know if the torment I was putting myself through was going to be worth it. In a hope of getting someone else's opinion I asked Zoe if she would read it for me.

I was feeling pretty good and really quite proud of my achievement so far, and still with a few days until my review with the specialist, I decided to actually do some research into publishing a book. It was clear to me that if I was serious about this, I would need to pay a good editor to sort out my grammar. That wouldn't be too much of a problem as long as my review went okay.

The specialist was again very business-like in his examination but it all went well. I had regained all the sensation in my arms and had a full range of movement without any pain. When he showed me my latest x-ray he said that everything had fused together well, and booked me in for a check-up in a few months' time.

"Any idea how long it will be before I can go back to work Doctor?" I asked as he gave me the date of the check-up.

"The sooner you get back to normal Mr Baily the better, so, you can go back when you feel you're ready for it." When he said that I could have jumped over the desk and kissed him. I held back though; instead, as soon as I was outside I phoned the office to say I'd had the all clear to come back. They gave me a start date two weeks away. I knew then that I'd made it.

Zoe's comments on my book left me a lot of work to do. She also now knew the full extent of what I was going through, so we spent a lot of time chatting online about it. I found it easy to talk to her that way, maybe because it was all in text and somehow unreal. It also showed me different ways to write the same thing, and with that I started to edit out the foul language from my manuscript where I could.

Work were very supportive when I did return. After arranging an advance in my wages to get me through to payday, and some hard graft to do, my appetite soon returned and I started to regain some weight. Then one of the guys asked what I'd been doing for the last six months, so, I told him I'd written a book.

He was instantly surprised, if not a little impressed, and after giving him a brief outline he asked if he could read it. I didn't know him very well but I agreed and emailed my manuscript across to him.

He thought it was brilliant and every few days for weeks after, he would ask me something about what had happened here and there in the story. I soon realised I shouldn't be telling him the answers, rather, I should be writing them. Reading through it again I could see the huge gaps I'd left out.

So for a couple of hours each night I'd sit and read my manuscript, adding a little there, or try to explain that better. It took a couple of months before I was happy, and by the time I'd finished, I had rewritten the whole story without shedding a single tear. Well that's a lie really but the tears were for the right reasons.

By now, I had also caught up with my rent arrears and the debt collectors where getting their regular payments again, allowing me to free up some cash. With that I sent my final draft off to the editors to work their magic. She actually did a fantastic job, though I wasn't overly impressed with what I got back at the time. But it did help to point out more holes so it was well worth it.

The only people to have read my efforts so far had been people I knew, admittedly some of the not very well, but, all the same, they wouldn't say anything bad about the book to me directly. But since the edit had taken six weeks to complete, I already had enough money spare again to send my manuscript off to a professional critique.

For the weeks that followed I was always on edge waiting for her report. I needn't have worried myself sick over it though, because after reading how well I'd written such a strong and powerful story it just left three bad points.

First was the biggest but the easiest to explain. It's a tough market for a book with this subject matter, and, I would have a great deal of trouble finding a publisher to take it on. Well it's my name on the cover, and you've just read my book, so I crossed that bridge eventually.

The other two I really needed to sort out straight away though, it was too short and didn't really have an ending. It was a setback for me, but at that time the story ended as I passed basic training. That gave me a lot of scope to raise my word count to a reasonable amount.

That was also the best advice I could have got, and within days of starting the extra chapters I could see that if I was going to write my memoirs, I needed to write all of them. From the beginning, right to the bitter end.

It took a few weeks to get a reasonable draft of my Army years together. I did find it much more enjoyable though, and again I learnt a lot about why I'm the person I am. Once I was done I sent it back to my critique for a re-read.

I got the shock of my life two days later when she phoned and introduced herself. From my research this was a rarity. So, she was going to tell me to stop harassing her, or, I was going to be an author.

"I just wanted to update you in person before I sent my report on Dave. Have you got a few minutes?" she asked. I said I did and she continued, "Well the first thing I wanted to say is the grammar in your later chapters needs an awful lot of attention."

"Yeah I know, but, as you've probably picked up I didn't make it to school that much. I do have plans to get it proofread and sort the grammar out. I just wanted to know if I was on the right track first because it could get quite expensive otherwise." I explained my plans for the future.

"That's fully understandable and a lot of authors do it the same way at this early stage." She said, and continued, "Well with that out of the way, what is there left to say but, *WOW*!"

The way she was talking I knew, she had generally enjoyed reading about my life, and for the next two hours we talked about the book. Knowing from her website that she once held a senior position for a broadsheet newspaper, I couldn't have got off to a better start.

During our chat she must have guessed that I also didn't have a clue what to do next, because, along with my report she added loads of information about the way to approach agents; she even wrote a synopsis and cover letter for me. Then the last line of my report basically said I still had more work to do stating, 'and for god's sake find an ending.'

We'd talked a lot about this on the phone but I still didn't have a clue what to do. I classed myself as still recovering from depression so, the only ending I could think of was to be published.

But staying as truthful as possible, I could only do that after it had happened, and then it would be too late to write about it. Other than that it would be to start the new life I'd promised myself from the royalties the book would bring in.

By now I'd caught up with all my bills, so in reality I had already started the latter, so I started to look for somewhere else to live, eventually settling on the Midlands. Once I'd settled in I had a look for a new job and soon found something a less stressful while I finished writing.

Work on the book progressed well, as short stories were added, closing a few more holes. Slowly as I deleted the randomness, and tweaked the language, a story started to come through, but an ending always eluded me.

I am very good at what I do for a living so, I earn a good wage. I don't want for anything and if there's a knock at the door I know my pizza is ready. It's a good life and I enjoy living this way but it's no happy ending to a book.

Then out of the blue I recognized the name of an old friend on Facebook. Not just any old mate I'd met in the Army in some far off land. This was the oldest friend it was possible for me to have, Lilly-Ann, the girl who encouraged me to swim.

Of course I couldn't be sure at first, because I hadn't seen her for so long, but of all the people in the world, she is the one I have thought of most often throughout my life. Mainly because every single time I've been asked where I learnt to swim, she has come to mind, screaming that she won't like me if I fail.

So I plucked up the courage and asked if she remembered me. She did of course, or I wouldn't be telling you about it, and soon we were talking regularly and friendships were made. Then I ran into a problem.

There's only so much you can say over the phone, and even with the book nearly written, there was still more to tell. So I wanted to meet her and talk; but that would mean a trip back home.

In all fairness, I wanted to show off when I booked the hotel, and with money to spare again, I know how to show off I can tell you. So I booked myself a night in one of the grandest hotels in the country, just a few miles from my childhood home, and invited Lilly-Ann to dinner.

As the luxury car I'd hired for the trip down was being valet parked, a porter carried my bags to my room for the night. Then, after a quick call to say that I'd arrived, Lilly-Ann joined me in the music room with the cream of society, and we talked like old mates do over afternoon tea.

She told me how she had always loved swimming and had gone on to become a County Champion before working as a lifeguard. Then, after reminding me that her mum taught me how to sew when I was a kid, I chatted to her about my book and my plans to have it published.

A couple of hours later, with the ice broken, Lilly-Ann left to get ready for the evening. Don't tell her, but I watched the end of the Rugby before I retired to my suite to pamper myself.

Formally dressed later that evening, I met Lilly-Ann in the music room for pre-dinner canapés. We chatted about her happy life, now a loving mother and dedicated wife. A short time later, we were escorted into a restaurant were the future King of England had eaten just the week before. Then we were treated to one of the finest dining experiences of my life.

After dinner we relaxed on a sofa by the bar, and as the pianist tapped away on his ivory's, I talked about my childhood for the first time. I would love to say that I told Lilly-Ann everything but I can't, there's just too much to say. Even so, when we joined a few other guests in the formal sitting room for a nightcap, I would say I had told her enough. And we were both smiling.

All the wine and rich food then went to my head, and I couldn't help taking Lilly-Ann on a guided tour of the mansion before she left. As we walked I talked about the fine art we passed it like I owned the place. I thought I was doing a pretty good job until her fits of giggles started.

On our way back to the reception she stood at the top of the grand staircase. So I lifted her onto the banister and held her hand as she slid down to the lobby. Then as I escorted her to a waiting Limo, she turned and said, "I'm proud of you Dave." And that night I had a dream for the first time that I can remember.

The following morning it felt like someone had just taken the weight of an eighteen stone bloke from my shoulders. And later, at breakfast my mind drifted back

to my book.

It had only been dinner as friends with Lilly-Ann the night before, so no love story to follow, however, it was still going to be my happy ending. A flamboyant departure from the hell I once called home, the boy did good, that kind of thing. But as I was mulling it over I saw more than just an ending for a story. With only a few more steps, I could get closure on that part of my life, a true ending.

A few hours later I took a drive around the town, stopping at various places that brought back memories. A lot's changed, but even with my old schools knocked down and rebuilt I still recognised them. The field where Andy died, that has had flats built on it now, though all my old childhood homes still look the same from the outside.

As I stood in front of one of them, the owner came out, asking me what I was doing. I said that I'd lived there some thirty years earlier, and I was just reminiscing to help with a book project. Kindly, he invited me in for a coffee, and a chat about the old times. I politely declined – not everyone needs to know my secrets.

The final step I made was at the local registry office. I asked how I go about changing my name. The receptionist handed me a few forms to fill out, and telling me the cost. I had to nip out and get them witnessed by my old doctor. Nonetheless, an hour later I handed them back with the fee, and left home for the last time, having learnt my final lesson from childhood.

It ended, when I became the man I am today.

Dave Baily died July 1983 aged 12 years, 7 months, 3 weeks and 4 days. As near as he can remember to the day they took Sarah, Clare and his room away from him, he has asked for nothing else since.

He died hoping people would understand that he tried to forget the past and protect the only thing he didn't care for: Himself.

The soldier stood and faced his God,
Which must always come to pass.
He hoped his shoes were shining,
just as brightly as his brass.

"Step forward now you soldier,
how shall I deal with you?
Should I turn the other cheek?
Or to My Church have you been true?"

The soldier squared his shoulders to repent,
"No, my Lord and Master, I guess I ain't.
Because some of us who carried guns;
Well, I couldn't always be a saint.

I've worked a lot of Sundays,
and at times my talk was tough.
And sometimes Sir, I've been violent,
because my world was awfully rough.

Though, I've never taken a penny,
that wasn't mine to keep,
but I've worked a lot of overtime,
when the bills got too steep.

And in this my Lord, my heart is true,
For never will I pass a cry for help,
though at times I'll shake with fear.
And please, my Father, forgive me,
for I've wept unmanly tears.

I know I don't deserve a place,
among the people here.

They never wanted me around them,
unless to calm their fears.

But if you've a place for me my Lord,
it needn't be so grand.
For I've never had, or wanted so much,
but if you don't, I'll understand.

There was a silence around the throne,
where the saints do often tread.
As the soldier waited quietly,
be it for it good or for his dread.

"Step forward now you soldier,
you've borne your burdens well.
Walk peacefully on Heaven's streets,
for my son, you've done your time in Hell.

I am now Dave White, the son I became. I'll talk about
Dave Baily, my brother, but I'm not him anymore. I hope
you understand why.

Clare,

Dave did want to say goodbye himself, but to see you in person he knew he couldn't. He was a good man in the end and would have kept you safe no matter the cost to himself; it was all he knew how to do. So just a few words if you'll indulge me.

He loved you for what you did for him back in the day, and all the good times you had together. Not that he remembers the good times much now days, he just knew he had them with you.

Then through the years that he thought you were dead, you still seemed to be there for him somehow. It made him want to be better than anyone else, so when he finally met his end you would meet him at heaven's door. Then, when he saw you alive and well, it made him even more determined to earn his place by your side.

For that he would like to thank you, because whenever it really did get too much for him, somehow, you always came to the rescue. Whether that was in thought or person he never said. He's also very sorry that he couldn't let you go, but without his room the only other place he felt safe was by your side.

And with that he wishes you well in whatever you may do, same for the kids of course.

He will always love you xXx

Life Without . . . My Father

by

The son I became

Born November 1980 aged almost 10

On behalf of

Dave Baily

You have told, now may your mind be at peace

By the son I became

10031911R00155

Printed in Great Britain
by Amazon.co.uk, Ltd.,
Marston Gate.